For Jacob

Or 'Smiley', as his Granddad calls him…

…and that's because his Granddad doesn't live
with him every day ;o)

SHARYN HAYDEN

I FORGOT TO TAKE MY PILL!
An Honest Diary Of A First-time Mum

CONTENTS

Prologue
VAGINAL TRICKERY

A friend of mine once drunkenly confessed that she had deliberately gotten pregnant. As in, she got pregnant on purpose without the express consent of the, you know, *owner of the sperm*. Their relationship had been wavering between being on, and off, and then on again for a few years and so she elected to take matters into her own hands. Or, in this case - into her own vagina.

I clearly remember all of the details she relayed to me that night: they were in Spain on holidays (where else would an Irish person go?), and on the very last night, she broke out the Irresistible Ride Me Now Dress.

She made sure to get both of them completely pickled drunk and then shagged him senseless on an otherwise unoccupied pool table, while an English drag queen called bingo numbers in the pub next door.

It was that kind of steamy, protection-free sex that makes babies, she said. And whadda you know, a few weeks later she was knocked up and by the time of this confession, they had a one-year-old.

'Er, really?' says I. 'And what did you tell him at the time? Like, how did you explain it?'

I was, frankly, a bit unsure as to whether or not I should really be hearing this at all. I mean, isn't that one of the worst clichés in the world about women – 'She Got Pregnant To Trap A Man'? (a nearby cousin, in the cringe factor, to 'She Got Her Boobs Done To Keep Her Fella Happy').

And here I was, sharing a plate of nachos and a few glasses of wine, with at least one woman who was living proof that the weird urban legend exists?

'I told him I was pregnant of course,' my friend slurred as she poured the last of the bottle of wine into our glasses - most of it into hers and some of it right there onto the bar table.

'But what did you tell him about how you got pregnant?' I pushed.
'Oh that.' She waved her hand dismissively as if this part of the story wasn't the most important bit. 'I just told him I forgot to take my pill, is all. D'ya have any smokes?'

My friend doesn't smoke. But then, I hadn't taken her for a vaginal man-trapper either. I might note that said one-year-old baby hadn't slept for the year since his arrival and her 'Zero-To-Drunkenness-ometer' was way low, an unfortunate side effect to sleep deprivation - but hence, I guessed, this amazing disclosure.

The mere whiff of a night out on the tiles for parents can make the most orderly of individuals conduct themselves in a manner that can only result in complete mortification (And from what I hear, often times with the neighbours. Nothing like telling the person that you have to live next door to forever, that you would be totally open to the concept of Swinging.

'Juss say the worddddd,' you slur at them, thinking you're winking when in fact your eyes have been closed for the last ten minutes).

Conscious as I was of my friend's fragile and wine-soaked state on that Night of Unsolicited Confessions, I was still dismayed by her. I mean, whatever happened to 'The Rules' or 'Men are from Mars...' and all of that shite. Don't call him first; when he does leave a message, wait X amount of time before calling back, never be too available etc.

Nowhere in those handbooks does it suggest, 'If he has continued commitment issues, use your uterus as leverage, fill it with a baby, and force said man to co-parent that baby with you for the rest of your lives. That'll learn him.'

I hope it's obvious that I'm not endorsing her approach in any way, but I have to tell you that my friend did end up marrying this guy and they actually really do love each other. That is, I assume, because her husband is not, and never will be, privy to this act of vaginal trickery.

But here's a little tip, a smidgeon of moral advice that I would glean from this story and pass on to you: the next time you find yourself in a relationship that isn't going so great, there's no need to get all pregnant on the situation.

Just be detached, like Beyonce when her little sister was beating the shite out of Jay Z in the lift that time, and insist on some time apart. My holistic advice for supreme emotional wellbeing is to crack one off daily to a Johnny Depp movie of your choice. That'll make you feel better and your fella will come running back eventually. I guarantee it*.

*Disclaimer: I do not guarantee anything. I have no idea what I'm talking about at the best of times.

chapter one
DAISY TRUMPS WILLY

Firstly, let me say this, I am a **big** fan of vagina. I like having one, I like using the word in conversation as much as possible ('And how is one's vagina? Is your vagina getting a seeing to? Has your vagina started talking to you yet? etc.).

It's something of a triumph for women, I think, to have this amazing anatomical area that multi-functions on a regular basis and that men are completely perplexed yet simultaneously fascinated with.

It's the divide between heterosexual men and women; women are very vagina-conscious, what with it being so *industrious* all the time, with the sex and the reproduction and the personal maintenance that it requires. Men, on the other hand, don't know what the fuck is going on down there and mostly don't want to know.

Beautifully, women are also armed with various, what I like to call get-out-of-jail 'Gee Cards' if they so choose to use them.

'Any chance of a ride, love?'

'Oh, sorry, sweetheart, I can't tonight.'

'What, headache?'

'No, actually, I didn't mention it because I didn't want to freak you out, but I had a little trouble *down there* recently, so I went to the doctor and – '

'Grand, grand. Actually, I'm not feeling great myself all of a sudden either. No worries, I'll just grab a beer. Do you want something from the kitchen, err…a hot water bottle perhaps?!' *peeling from the room at lightning speed to the farthest spot in the house, to recover composure and praying that he won't be asked to go to the shop for tampons*

Getting out of sex is just one ridiculously easy feat, and it's not that we're not into having sex; believe me, we are. But there are reasons why we might be evasive; for example, we may have just paid for an expensive fake tan application that we don't want to have destroyed with willy-shaped white bits, you know?

Or we waited so long for you to come to bed that we, ahem, 'entertained ourselves' with a scene recalled from a Hugh Jackman movie. Any Hugh Jackman movie. What I'm saying is, you stayed up too late watching *The Walking Dead* downstairs and missed your ridie window. It's that simple.

The whole idea of discussing anything to do with one's vagina, apart from saying, 'Everything's fine, am completely available to shag' is seemingly so uncomfortable for certain men, that I think us women could literally get away with anything.

1. Need milk but can't face getting into the car to go to the shops?

'I have horrible cramps today, could you go and I'll pop the kettle on for tea when you get back.' (You can definitely get that tea made for you if you also wedge in some light 'cramp-related' audible moaning on his return.

Just lock yourself in the downstairs loo and do it from there so he can't see your face as you try not to piss yourself laughing).

2. Need some time alone on a Saturday night and don't want to go meet all his mates in the pub after the rugby/soccer/GAA match?

'Oh I'd love to, but I think I'm getting my period and will probably tell your mate Jonathon's girlfriend that he cheated on her on Seán's stag, just because I'm feeling a bit, you know, irrational.'

3. Need the bathroom to yourself for an hour?

'I have my period darling. It's all a bit, you know, "vagina" today.'

4. Have to visit the mother-in-law?

'Vagina.'

5. Your turn to drop the kids off at school?

'Vagina.'

6. Walk the dog?

'Vagina.'

Vagina. Vagina. Vagina.

Vagina *rocks*.

I grew up in a house with three younger brothers, so I wasn't really aware that I had a vagina until I was about ten. I mean, I knew I peed from somewhere, and I distinctly remember one of my pals on the street telling me that hers was called a 'Daisy', and so

I went along with that. But it wasn't really something I had to think about.

We lived on a great street in a seaside town in Dublin called Rush, where nothing but fields of muck greeted us in the area facing our row of houses, and they provided a cool playground.

There were verrry slight bumps in that muck that we liked to call 'hills', bless us, presumably because they were so much bigger than our ten-year-old selves.

Boys and girls from the neighbourhood liked to congregate there, planning who was going to be in the next bike race, who was barred from Rounders for being rubbish at it, and who I would deem worthy to be in my next production of *Sharyn Hayden presents Ireland's New Kids On The Block!* (One of my three brothers was invariably cast on account of being related to the 'director', even though I'm not sure that they ever willingly auditioned, to be honest).

It was on these hills of muck that I first realised that boys and girls were very different, when Martin, sandy blonde, tall and gangly, pulled me aside and tried to tell me that Santa wasn't real.

I stood with my arms folded and squinted at him for a few minutes, deciding what I could possibly do with this information.

Would I run home to my mother and ask her if it was true? Would I interrogate him for some factual information to back up his slander? Would I march him to my house to show him the precise point on my bedroom window where Rudolf the Red-Nosed Reindeer had, in fact, rested his weary paws the Christmas previous?

Nope. I decided there and then on a different course of action: I kicked him straight in the bollox.

What ensued was utter pandemonium, as Martin blanched whiter than white and collapsed face down into a crumpled heap, knees, chest and face covered in muck.

The other neighbourhood kids rushed to his aid, asking him what had happened, but poor Martin could only mutter incomprehensible squeaks.

He had gone from being Mr. Mouthy Know-It-All to a babbling mess with one swift kick of my BROS-inspired steel-toed boots (And seriously, on reflection – OUCH).

The congregated crowd eventually decided on the most extreme course of action - the very last resort when kids are in trouble: someone was sent up the road to get his mother.

As every brave balls-kicking ten-year-old girl would, I scurried back home as fast as my pale, chubby, freckled legs would take me and refused to be drawn into any conversation about how playtime was.

'Did you have fun?' my mam said.
 'Oh yes, plenty, thanks.'
'Why have you come straight up to your room?'
 'I, erm, wanted to clean it?'

Suspicious. Or. What.

Approximately ten minutes later, Martin, with a little more colour in his cheeks (and considerably more in his bollox, I would wager) and his mother were knocking at our front door.

I had observed their approach through the curtains of my bedroom window, and every step they took filled me with more and more dread. I was panicking, sweating, wondering if my Barbie gym had any magic powers that would somehow help me to disappear. Surely that weird contraption had to be good for something. Argh! I knew I was going to be in big trouble.

'Sharyn! Get down here!'

Not one to mess with The Mammy when she is taking *that* tone, I hurtled myself downstairs to the hallway, where Martin's own mammy was presenting the injured pre-pubescent soldier.

Even though poor Martin looked suitably mortified and wouldn't make eye contact with any of us, he was still unable to de-cup his hands from his crotch and continued to hang on for dear life.

'Sharyn,' my mother hissed, 'you can't go around kicking boys like that. Martin has a willy and they can be very *sore*. You better apologise right now.'
'Erm, sorry, Martin,' I mumbled.

Mine and Martin's mammy exchanged looks of, 'Ok, well that's that sorted then.' (Sadly gone are the days when kids scrapped with each other and no one had to get sued and/or be tweeted about acrimoniously).

I remember looking at Martin and I did genuinely feel sorry. And then I felt really sorry for *him.* Not only had I kicked him really hard, but he had a willy too. A willy! Outrageous misfortune.

Later that night in my bedroom, I sat down to write a very important letter:

'Dear Santa,
For Christmas this year, please can Martin have a Daisy? I think I may have broken his willy...'

Chapter Two
STUPID IS AS STUPID PROCREATES

Having kids wasn't something that was ever top of my agenda when I was growing up. In fact, I don't think the notion crossed my mind that much at all. I was far too busy planning my hairdressing business/writing songs/learning every single word to *The Sound of Music* for that kind of lark.

But that's not to say that I never wanted to have kids either. Of course somewhere in my mid-to-late twenties, when I was in the middle of crazy, crazy love with *WhatsHisNameNow* all we talked about was having imaginary babies together.

'Ohmigod, I love you.'
 'Ohmigod, I love you too. Our babies will be so beautiful.'
'I know. How many babies will we have?'
 'As many as possible. Let's just have a big house and loads of babies. Babies coming out of the rafters. And you'll be so beautiful pregnant!'
'I will! Ohmigod. Ohmigod.'

These conversations obviously happened during sex, when one is most alert in one's genital area and most stupid in one's brain box. When ridiculous promises were made of,

'Promise me you'll come on a cruise with my grandparents in August.'

'I promise!'

And dreams akin to winning the Lotto were planned:

'I'll train as a barrister and we'll live in New York!'

'Yes!'

'You'll never have to work again!'

'Yes! Yes! Yes!'

Then, after the big, sad, uber-drawn-out breakup, all that remained to see anywhere you could think to go, were truly happy and chic-looking couples with adorable, smiling kids. And then you'd *really* want them, but only with the bastard who'd most recently ripped your heart out. It's like some sort of twisted Karmic torture that is forced upon post-separate-ways single folk.

There is literally no place safe in the world where you will not be presented with some happy child or other, that you will spend the next week bawling over, drinking wine over and (scarlet) texting ex-boyfriend over. *The 3am Babies That Could Have Been Text Messages.*

I even had to flee a nightclub once, on the basis that there was a happy baby staring back at me. But to be fair, the club was a shithole in North County Dublin and to be doubly fair, I'm pretty sure that baby was hammered. So not the greatest example of what I'd hoped for my future Little Ones.

What did I really know about having babies in my twenties anyway? I admit to being what you would call, a 'Late Bloomer' in many respects. My childhood seems to have happily extended into my teens and beyond, rendering me akin to a teenager in my twenties and now like a twenty-something in my thirties. Everyone else my age around me (and some younger, I may add) just seem so mature and clever and use big words by comparison.

I attribute my childlike and constant immature state to two things:

1: I am a total dreamer who is prone to drifting off and blocking out large chunks of conversations/events/the entire day sometimes, due in part to re-running the season finale of *Will & Grace* in my head (What. Were. They. THINKING?). And otherwise just making mental lists of whose mortgages to pay off when I win the EuroMillions. And,

2: I'm not entirely sure that I am all that well educated, for an educated girl.

With reference to Point Number One, I can only say that I was born that way: an artist, a diva, or 'a little bitch' as my uncle Larry would call it (He babysat me on several occasions so his first-hand account is totally accurate).

To prove this point – and not that you would need proof if you knew me – I remember precisely nothing from junior school apart from being in the school play. I can still remember the lines, 'Up the hill and down the lane', as I gestured with great dramatic flair towards the 'Up', and greater dramatic flair towards the 'Down' in my baby blue leotard. I remember it clear as a bell. I was three.

Need more? Ok, I remember nothing from my first day at a new school in North County Dublin either, aside from pulling pieces of chalk from my dolly suitcase, stuffing them into my crazy over-smiling mouth and announcing to everyone that I loved cheese. I was five.

I assume you'll take me at my word.

On Point Number Two, the feeling of ignorance – well it wasn't for the want of trying, let me tell you. I mean, I went to five primary and secondary schools collectively (yes, multiples, there was an issue with me acting too much like 'One of the lads' in a co-ed secondary school and so my parents shoved me face-first into an all-girls school in the end). And I went to college. Yes, since you ask, I did do an arts degree because no, I had no idea what I wanted to do with my life. Other than act and the drama programme at Trinity College Dublin said no. Twice. The fuckers.

I sought guidance from the counsellor in secondary school once who, after several aptitude (AKA waste of time) tests later, deduced that I would make a great mechanic. A *mechanic*. This is to the now thirty-seven-year-old who still doesn't know how to put air into her car tyres.

Is it any wonder then, that one went on what can only be described as a rampage of evening courses after said arts degree to figure out one's path in life? We're talking every single evening course in the evening course book. So many, I could possibly be a serial student. I reckon my problem is that I can't quite figure out what I'm interested in precisely, aside from telling you that I'm just kind of interested in everything.

Therefore, I know lots of little bits about bits of things, but fuck all on any one particular subject.

For example, I have paid good money for and received various qualifications (that are in a box under the bed somewhere), for the following courses:

1. A Certificate in The Performing Arts (I recall particularly enjoying being a slug for an entire day. Essentially, you just sleep off your hangover whilst pressed face-first against the wall).

2. A Diploma in Communications and PR (I wanted to drink free champagne and eat tiny cheese and crackers at boring, forgettable events. I had no money and needed to be fed).

3. A Diploma in Legal Studies (I wanted to be Ally McBeal. In *Ally McBeal*)

4. Beauty Therapy (I give the worst fake tan jobs imaginable. You'd honestly be better off booking in for a session with Katie Price).

5. Web Design (Waaaay too late in the game & seriously not technically minded enough. I can just about navigate through WordPress).

6. Acting Classes (I wanted to be in *Love/Hate*, but only if I could write a female role who didn't want to get fucked at the back of a bin shed by all the drug dealers)

7. TV Presenting (I wanted to interview Hugh Jackman through the medium of song and dance. And maybe snogging).

You could be forgiven for thinking that all of my efforts here would result in my having a bit of cop on. But not so, my friends, not so.

By the time I got pregnant at thirty-four, for example, I still wasn't entirely sure what the difference was between my cervix and my pelvis. I had no idea that the growing pains I experienced while my body was expanding did not mean I was having a heart attack; that forms need to be filled out IN GOOD TIME in order to receive maternity benefit when you really need it; that agreeing to perform in a highly physical theatre show five weeks after the baby's due date is nothing short of lunacy, or that having a baby is really, really hard.

But then, that is coming from the girl who, at twelve, tried to use a tampon for the first time and stuck it in the place where the wee comes out. Several times over.

Fact.

Chapter Three
BUGGY NINJA

It was while visiting my younger brother and his pregnant wife in the UK one November that I got 'The Goo', and it took me completely by surprise. My intention was really only to see how their Bump was progressing and make sure my brother wasn't being a useless git.

I have three brothers and they're all excellent men (well reared by Mammy Hayden), but it is the job of the older sister to make sure they are treating their ladies as they should be treated. Just as it is my brothers' job to take hurling sticks 'round the house of any guy that is treating their sister badly. It's ok if we slag each other off, but no one else can, capiche?

Yep, that's us Haydens. We're like the Sibling Mafia. We fight with each other all the time but we're madly protective of each other too. Basically, we should live in The Bronx and Ben Affleck should be our baseball hoodie-wearing neighbour who cuts our grass from time to time.

This trip to the UK was important, too, because no one in our family had ever expected a baby before. It was the first grandchild and we were all just a teeny tiny bit over-excited about the prospect of the new addition. We took it all VERY seriously; my mother and I even took up knitting, and happily bestowed mismatched and unevenly shaped baby cardigans and booties on the future parents.

The big bummer was that my brother had moved to Leeds some years previously, and that's where this new baby would be born. We were all stuck in Dublin being excited about the imminent arrival via Skype, which sucked (Although I'm pretty sure Shane and Claire were only too relieved to have a bit of distance between them and us mentallers).

There was shopping to be done in Harrogate the weekend I visited: baby shopping. The three of us trundled off to have a look at buggies. A wonderful sales assistant lady instantly came to help us and offered a demonstration as to how their fantastic range worked. I will never forget watching Shane and Claire's faces as the look of utter horror and confusion ultimately engulfed them during the demo.

And they weren't alone – my face was doing its 'What The Fuck?!' routine too. If you have ever seen a ninja move, perhaps scaling a series of ten-foot walls and rooftops in an effort to escape the scene of a crime, you might have a visual on the speed that this sales assistant operated.

She flicked buggies up and down, gadget on, gadget off, parasol up, parasol down, drinking cup holder on, drinking cup holder off, with pram, with detachable car seat, music on, seatbelts tightened, three wheel, four wheel, different colours – reds, blues, Disney themed - at such great speed that all of our heads were spinning.

How the hell were they supposed to pick the right one, I wondered? How were they supposed to know exactly what the best thing to do for their future baby was?

Clearly, I was no expert, but I had taken public transport for many, many years, and during that time, had seen several mothers and fathers struggling to get on the bus or train with kids, bags and the contraptions that ferried the kids around. I even had a kid shoved in my direction to hold once or twice, when a buggy was being particularly awkward.

These memories came flooding back as I stood, stunned, and thought to ask the only important question I could think of:

'Em, where are the, you know, one-handed buggies please?'

My brother and his wife diverted their attentions to stare blankly at me. Claire, presumably, because she was still stunned from the Ninja Buggy Demo and Shane in that sibling 'Oh fuck off with your annoying, interfering questions, sis', kind of way.

The sales assistant looked nervous, and I'm fairly certain, did a quick head-to-toe body scan to make sure my extremities were still all in order before asking, 'I'm not sure what you mean?'

Shane was pleading with me with his forehead at this point, all crinkled up in a 'Don't take the piss' furrow. I ignored him, as I usually do.

'Say for example, Claire has her baby on one hip and is holding on tight. Now she needs to open the car boot to get her little bag of shopping from Morrisons in, before folding the buggy and putting that in the boot before getting baby into the car seat inside. Where are the buggies that can be easily folded and opened up again with her one free hand?'

Another silence, but not on our side this time. Success! The sales assistant looked gutted to be faced with such a reasonable question, stuttered around her non-answer and I left my brother there to bask in my brilliance. I strutted off to have a look at some other items that I could buy for Christmas presents, giving myself an Air Five as I went.

There were a few other babies in my life at the time as some friends had been busy reproducing. I lay my hands on a reindeer-styled onesie with a cute furry bottoms and the tiniest snowman booties you have ever seen, and something strange happened in my womb. It did a... a kind of flip.

Fobbing it off as probably related to the huge pub lunch I'd just had, I ignored it.

Popping over to the Early Learning section, I went on the hunt for a few educational toys for the older kids in my life. I mean, Play-Doh wouldn't make my steak and kidney pie come back up, would it?

As I attempted to select some very practical art sets, the kind that cool aunts are famous for, I was disabled by something in the corner of my eye: glitter.

My favourite thing.

Inner drag queen engaged, I was rooted to the spot as my gaze sought out the source of this magical, twinkling matter. Before I knew what was happening my eyes landed at the kiddie clothes rail. I wasn't quick enough to turn away and would never undo my seeing it: a tiny, beautiful, glittery pink and purple fairy princess dress.

And right there, right in the middle of the baby shop in Harrogate, Leeds, I started crying. For a good, highly embarrassing, ten minutes or so.

I whipped out the phone and texted my boyfriend of a couple of years, the very handsome, and appropriately nicknamed, Ass Monkey (you'll see why when you see a photo of him, honestly).

Me: Hiya. Having a great time, weather is shite but it is winter after all. I was wondering if you might be in the market to impregnate me when I get back?

Ass Monkey: Yeah, ok, cool.

Me: ARE YOU ACTUALLY SERIOUS???

Ass Monkey: Yeah, why the hell not?

Me: *Throws Pill In Bin* Love you xxx

When I returned to Ireland, the 'Great Freeze of 2010' was just upon us. The weather was so bad that businesses closed down, snow socks sales for car tyres went through the roof, and 'that' guy slipped on the ice and was featured on the nine o'clock RTÉ news before becoming a YouTube sensation.

The country was at a veritable standstill. Neither Ass Monkey nor I could get to work and erm, had to stay indoors a lot, keeping each other, you know, warm...

Christmas came around and we partied like rock stars, as was our way. I have this romantic idea of Christmas being my favourite time of the year ever, but with caveats attached. It is only perfect to me so long as nobody tries to wreck it with fights (which they usually do), and the Christmas tree isn't attacked by a dancing drunken uncle (Every. Single. Year).

But Christmas 2010 *was* a particularly good one, I remember. We spent Christmas Eve drinking with my brothers in various bars in my hometown. My sis-in-law Claire was with us, though heavily pregnant at that point, so probably hated us but was in great spirits.

Ass Monkey and I popped off home on Christmas Eve with our Santa Bags (my amazing mother still gives us bags for the end of our beds every year) and finished off the cooking and baking for Christmas dinner (One of the great things about Ass Monkey is that he's a wicked cook – I can actually burn soup – and he had elected to put Christmas dinner together that year. It. Was. Amazing).

On Stephen's Day, we always go to Ass Monkey's family and hang out with all the nieces and nephews and the millions of dogs that are running around.

They're a big dog family and that year, we had our own little puppy Pearl to add to the chaos. (She rewarded our inclusion of her with shitting and pissing all over the floors in every room, and we spent most of the day running around after her so that none of the kids would end up sticking their fingers (or faces) in it).

I cannot and will not, tell a word of a lie when I say that I probably drank the guts of a bottle of Bacardi between that day and night. We stayed over – no doubt because we absolutely had no chance of making it home by our own devices - and couldn't function for days afterwards but unusually, I was in a far worse state than Ass Monkey.

'And me with the benefit of youth on my side!' I kept protesting, roaring at him from beneath my New Kids On The Block duvet cover on the couch.

Then on New Year's Eve, I had this weird thought: *Shouldn't I have had my period by now?*

Which was followed by: *Oh my fucking jaysus!*

I ran to the pharmacy for a pregnancy test, brought it home to do that thing you do when you buy a pregnancy test and there it was: ***positive***.

On New Year's Eve 2010, Ass Monkey and I discovered that we'd made a baby. Just like that. Bob's your uncle and Fanny's your aunt.

Chapter Four
STUPID SHIT MY NEIGHBOUR SAYS

For some reason, perhaps resting within the realms of sadism, people just love to share awful horror stories with pregnant women and *especially* to women who are expecting their first baby.

You know that precise time when you're already terrified, resolutely refusing to dye your hair, drink anything with caffeine in it, lift or carry anything (that's a great one for getting out of the vacuum cleaning, by the way), or eat anything that's been in the fridge for longer than twelve hours? That's when they strike, the miserable bastards.

I was *so* lucky when I was pregnant in that I wasn't sick in any way (just had evil heartburn towards the end), or needed crutches like my friend Simsonite, who had a pain that she described as 'not unlike someone had actually kicked you straight in the gee.'

She had that for half of her pregnancy. That's TWENTY WEEKS. Which is FIVE WHOLE MONTHS. Please don't make me break it down into days for you, math gives me psoriasis.

So even though I had been thoroughly enjoying myself while pregnant, basking in the 'I can eat what I like, lie down and have a snooze when I like' glory of the whole process, there were certain people I encountered along the way who kind of tried to ruin it.

These were people who took huge pleasure in cocking their condescending faces to one side, employing their most annoying talking-to-a-mentally-challenged-person-tone, in order to say things like,

Cockface: 'Hi, how are you doing there, pregnant lady? Aren't you positively blooming?'
Me: 'Oh yes, doing great. The baby is healthy, I'm healthy, I'm actually really enjoying it all, thanks so much for asking.'
Cockface: 'Awww, that's great for you that you're feeling great now, yar yar. Just great (Put-on smile fades to reveal authentic face of bitter and twisted miserable bitch akin to Michelle Pfeiffer in Stardust when the youth serum wears off). I'm telling you now though, just wait until…'

…and they gleefully describe something horrific involving you and your newborn baby having to be airlifted to safety from the clutches of some pack of wolves or other.

To prevent me from unearthing my inner scumbag and punching anyone's face in, I ultimately took on board a policy of laughing my pregnant ass off whenever I was offered one of these 'pearls of wisdom' and tried not to take any of it too seriously.

When relaying these comments to Ass Monkey or any nice friends and family, I entitled this scaremongering as 'Stupid Shit My Neighbour Says'. I thought that gave it the jolly feel it so deserved (By the way, I used the term 'neighbour' in general terms, describing the people in my life and community and not to describe my actual next-door neighbour at the time). (Although not necessarily not her either).

Here's just a little example of the type of comments that I received upon sharing the good news that I was pregnant, and general unsolicited comments received relating to the upcoming (very exciting – to me!) birth of my child.

Director's Note: try your best to use the most irritating, whiny, bitter and twisted voice that your brain will conjure up as you read them, and you'll get the idea of what I had to endure. Side note: I am NOT making any of these up - I SWEAR.

1. 'Coming off the pill and getting pregnant straight away is really bad for the baby.' (This person knew that this is precisely how we got pregnant. Pill in bin, rampant riding, impregnated. Job done. I'd say I was off the pill all of five seconds. Thanks, asshole).

2. 'Oh you're pregnant! Congratulations! I nearly died during childbirth, and so did my sister. But erm, that won't happen to you.'

3. 'Are you dying with heartburn yet? No? You probably will be, mark my words. Keeps you awake all night long and sometimes you feel like someone shoved lighter fluid down your throat and then set a match to it.'

4. 'Wait until your organs start all pushing up against your ribcage. It hurts so, so, SOOOOO much. I thought I was suffocating to death when it happened to me.'

5. 'Pregnant, is it? Another little shit to add to the world then.' (**yes, really**)

6. 'Don't get your hopes up.' (This was when I was going for a scan to find out if we were having a boy or a girl. I WILL get my fucking hopes up if you don't mind!)

7. 'I know for a FACT that the use of second-hand mattresses for your baby cot or Moses basket leads directly to cot death.' (Where are you getting all of this 'factual' information from? And is this really from the woman who smoked twenty cigarettes a day when she was pregnant?)

8. 'Did you plan it?'

Number 8, without a shadow of a doubt, has to have been my favourite. I mean, Ass Monkey and I may not have pondered on the decision for very long (i.e. a couple of text messages and one drunken, loved-up lunch did the trick), but **we did make the decision to have a baby**. I was thirty-four and he was thirty-eight! We were extremely grown up and sensible and based our decision on the following information:

1. We (he) was getting on and we (he) didn't want to be an old parent (dad).

2. We didn't hate kids.

3. It would be an amazing experience to embark upon together.

4. We may only have been going out together for three (sometimes turbulent) years, but we were

friends before that for ten, so essentially we were enough of an old married couple to pull it off.

5. Everyone else was doing it.

6. We had gotten a dog in July and had managed to keep her alive thus far. A baby couldn't be that much different.

7. Even though Ass Monkey wasn't (and still isn't, unfortunately) black, I would still concur that he was the most handsome man I had ever met and I chose to procreate with him, and him only.

So we did (loosely) plan it. And is it anyone's business if we didn't anyway? What kind of question IS that to ask someone?

That's the kind of juicy information you stumble upon when you meet your friend from school at a wedding, who you haven't seen for fifteen years, and she blurts out, crying at 3am, 'I don't know how I'm pregnant. We haven't had sex in four years. The only thing I can think of is the Jacuzzi that time when I went to Lanzarote with the girls...waaaaaahhhh.'

That's the kind of information I'm into discussing. Unsolicited, Jeremy Kyle Show worthy info. But I'd never ask. Unless the baby to a very white Irish couple did actually come out black. Then I'd - at the very least - raise an eyebrow.

Things You Should Never Say To A Pregnant Woman

1. 'DOESN'T THAT FEEL AMAAAZING?'

…as you rub the bump you weren't invited to rub. Do you seriously not understand that a pregnancy bump isn't some sort of 'clip-on extension' to my body – it's an actual part of me that starts under my boobs and stops close to my vagina? My *vagina*.

If you insist on grabbing for it and rubbing the underside of the bump – at my vagina – with that ridiculous delighted-to-be-a-part-of-the-magic grin on your face, I'm going to have to shove my hand down your husband's pants the next time I see him. Same. Exact. Thing.

2. 'OH MY GOD YOU'RE HUGE!'

Are you joking me? I'm entirely exhausted from growing this person inside me as I carry on working/walking the dog/dealing with the increasingly demented staff at buggy retail outlets, I had to quit smoking – my favourite pastime – my Forever 21 sparkly mini dress now makes me look like Little Miss Sunshine when I try it on, no one will have sex with me (and believe me, I've asked everyone), I've just watched a video of a woman giving birth **in the seventies** at the maternity hospital, which I will never get over – and you want to tell me that I'm fat. Do you? *DO YOU?!*

3. 'ARE YOU STILL HERE?'

This can also masquerade as 'Have you not had that baby yet ha ha!', is a sacked employee of 'He's too happy in his mammy's tummy there, isn't he?' and a distant (weird) cousin of 'Is it your first? You'll probably go about two weeks over so.'

Like, who are you – some uterine cosmologist who specifically knows the course of my gestation period? And if so, where the fuck were you approximately (who can say, we were drunk a lot) forty weeks ago to tell him to put a frickin' condom on?

4. 'ANY IDEA WHO THE FATHER IS?'

Jaysus…

Chapter Five
MOTHER OF PEARL

I became a mother, for the first time, to a human boy child called Jacob on September 5th, 2011. Despite the fact that some stranger I encountered at the shops that morning, *did* roar at me, 'Is it your first? You'll be about two weeks over then!', I went into labour exactly a day before my due date. So *shove* it, Opinion Lady Freakazoid.

It was a funny day, that September 5th, as it had started off with our one and only staff member fucking off on us (Ass Monkey and I started an engineering firm pretty much the second I got pregnant. Sooo smart).

Once we'd lifted our jaws back up off the floor, that someone would be so arse-holey as to leave us in the lurch right when our baby was about to arrive into the world, I distracted myself from thoughts of murder with painting the ceiling of the bathroom.

Ass Monkey had been tormented for the duration of the pregnancy with my demands of 'Fix that!' 'Change this!' 'You're an engineer – figure it out!' and had, to be fair, transformed our two-bedroomed apartment into a gorgeous comfy home that any baby would have been delighted to rest their little head in.

There were just teeny tiny corners in the bathroom where the paintwork hadn't been finished and since he was busy lamenting his one and only helper on the road doing a runner, I decided to give him his five minutes and get busy finishing it myself.

It was while teetering on a chair, reaching up over my head with the smallest painter's brush, filling in the tiniest of gaps on the ceiling that no other human being would ever have noticed, that I felt a little… something in my back. It felt like a teeny tiny period pain, or if I'm honest, *a poo cramp*, but one that only lasted for a second.

Having had several aches and pains of varying degrees during the pregnancy, and not being due for another twenty-four hours at least, I ignored it and carried on, finishing the little task at hand.

About a half an hour later – another twinge. Hmmm…

'Honey, I don't mean to alarm you but…'
 'Yes?' he replied, not removing his eyes from the TV for even a millisecond.
'I'm pretty sure something is, you know, happening.'

There was a flicker in his eyes; something was clicking into place. I stood in the doorway, willing the TV to spontaneously combust and wishing I could send him telepathic messages from my preggo brain to his engineer's one: 'We're having a bayyyybeeeee. Remember, we're having a bayyyybeeee.'

Remote control in hand, Ass Monkey muted the TV screen (which is passive-aggressive for actually turning it off) and slowly, very slowly, turned his pretty little head towards me, recognition pending.

'We better go for chicken wings then,' he announced.

Although one might expect a woman in potential labour to have been disappointed at his reaction, enraged even, that he was displaying some sort of denial over the situation at hand, I honestly could not have been any prouder of him at that moment. My man, calm, cool and always in control of our culinary needs.

'Bloody great idea,' I agreed.

We took ourselves down to a fantastic place called Blue Bar which overlooks the harbour in Skerries. We scoffed their famous chicken wings and I had a glass of nerve-calming wine to accompany them. I was timing my 'incidents' with the stopwatch on my phone and they were now exactly every twenty minutes apart.

In between the shoving of grub into my gob, and chatting with Ass Monkey about what lay ahead of us, inwardly, I began to panic. That despite all the antenatal classes I went to, despite watching Super Nanny religiously at night when I couldn't sleep because of the bastard heartburn, despite reading every single piece of literature I could find on pregnancy, labour and birth, I had no idea what any of this meant right now!

When was I supposed to ring the hospital, when the contractions were ten minutes apart or ten minutes long? Surely they couldn't be ten minutes long, why the fuck would Mother Nature do that to anyone?

Should I be doing figure-of-eights on the fit ball just now instead of stuffing myself and making it impossible for the baby to find its way out through the mass of chicken and hot sauce and chips that I had just ingested and that I was sure would now be stuck in my intestine and wouldn't that be a barrier to an easy birth?

Had my waters broken and I hadn't noticed? How would I know? How the actual fuck was I supposed to know what was going on?

There was only one thing for it: I had to ring The Mammy.

'Hi, Mam. There's a good chance something is happening. It's not mad sore but it's no trip to the spa either. Every twenty minutes, Mam. HELP MEEEEE!'

Mammy Liz was already on her way over before I had even put the phone down: excellent work (She and I had secretly discussed her being in the labour room with me when I gave birth and were both very excited about the prospect, until we remembered the existence of Ass Monkey as a person and his very active role in these proceedings. We grumpily concluded that we should probably let him have his moment and be there himself for the birth of his first child. I was *genuinely* torn).

Maybe it was the wine, but Ass Monkey and I decided 'In for a penny, in for a pound' and stopped by an ice cream parlour for a couple of takeaway ice cream tubs en route to the car.

About halfway between the parlour and getting back home, I had the first tough pain. It lifted my arse clean off the car seat and almost caused me to spill my precious ice cream (but as someone who can hang on to the end of her Bacardi and Coke during a shitty plane landing, I am proud to say I didn't spill one hundred NOR one thousand). That was the first moment I truly knew: *This is happening. We're having a baby.*

Utter panic ensued. We weren't ready, I had no idea what was in the hospital bag, if our designated surrogate dog mother was available to come get our doggie Pearl overnight and OH MY GOD we forgot to bring back the DVD.

Within five minutes of arriving home, I was frog-marching Ass Monkey, Pearl and I up to the village to bring back that DVD, lest we should be seen to be anything other than upstanding citizens, even in times of acute stressful every-twenty-minute labour pains.

I believed I had it timed perfectly. I had a contraction before we left the house and so off we waddled on the journey that should only have taken ten minutes there and back, just in time for the next round of pain. Of course I wasn't at all taking into consideration that I was just about to pop and could no longer walk at a speedy pace. Waddly, preggo activity was all I could reasonably muster.

So you can imagine my complete mortification and shame that I did not make it to said DVD shop in one piece. I was almost there when I was struck down with another pain and yes, I endured it – doubled over a wall right there in the middle of the village that we lived in, red-faced and moaning like a newborn calf, for all to see.

When we finally got back to the apartment, I promised that I would now be good and get ready to go to the hospital, but I would like a bath first please. I had been to a friend's wedding the night before and had a full tan, nail varnish and fake eyelashes on. It was absolutely nothing to do with 'Labour Prep' or anything like it, honestly - just happy coincidence, my favourite kind.

We put the water on and got the bags in the car. Liz (praise be!) arrived and surveyed the situation. Ass Monkey's sister Naomi, who was being a legend and taking Pearl for a week on her 'holidays', was notified.

'Oh yes, you're definitely in labour,' my sage mother nodded as I collapsed over the couch one more time with a contraction that rendered me temporarily incapable of speaking to anyone.

'You think?' I eventually breathed. I mean, what gave it away, Ma...?!

'Em Sharyn?' Ass Monkey intervened. He is the manly silent type under normal stressful circumstances but on this particular evening, I remember him being mostly my fellow-deer-caught-in-the-headlamps type.

(He was the stag and I was the doe and we had just escaped The Phoenix Park under cover of darkness, only to find ourselves faced with the last bus to Ballyfermot, recently hijacked by a couple of lads hoping to make it back to the pub on time for last orders. Same. Exact. Facial Expressions).

We hadn't a clue what we were doing and we were bleedin' terrified.

'Your contractions are coming every eight minutes now.'
 'WHAT?!' (That was me and Liz simultaneously).
'You won't get a bath now, you better go,' she guided us.

I started to cry. Obviously.

 'I know, I know, it's scary but you're going to be fine,' she soothed.
'It's not that,' I wiped my snots and tears into her handy always-up-the-sleeve tissue that she had given me.
 'What is it then?' Ass Monkey asked impatiently, one foot inside the apartment and one foot wedging the front door ajar. 'We. Have. To. Go!'

I stopped sobbing like a baby for long enough to admit, 'I don't want to leave Pearl behind.'

Ass Monkey immediately got on to his sister Naomi to confirm her ETA.

'She'll be here to take Pearl in twenty minutes, max' he promised.

I know they both thought I was bananas, and maybe I was, but at that moment, leaving my gorgeous puppy Pearl behind without Naomi right there to love her as much as I normally would wasn't an option.

My mother, who isn't exactly the biggest fan of dogs, had to swear and double swear that she wouldn't leave the house until Naomi came to take her as Ass Monkey dragged me out the door. I mean, who foregoes potential adequate medical care for the birth of their first child in lieu of staying behind in the house to ensure their puppy is taken care of?

I do, ok?! *I do.*

As a perfect Pearl Mammy, I had our doggie all packed for her week's 'holidays' with a pink (knock off) Louis Vuitton bag, stuffed with food, toys and treats. It also contained a lovely letter to her aunty Naomi which explained that she would be no trouble as a houseguest…

…Em, yes, I typed and printed out that letter to Naomi on Pearl's behalf. As If I were Pearl. The dog. The Dog Pearl.

Oh God, I was Pearl's unpaid ghostwriter.

Ah look, I was pregnant and out of my mind, ok? Can you stop judging me for just a second *PLEASE?!*

Wait. I've just remembered that I made Pearl do a little mucky paw-print on the end of the page – to make the letter authentic.

Ok fuck it. Judge away. I SO deserve it.

Dear Aunty Naomi,

Hi, Pearl here. You may have heard I'm a bit of a bitch but mostly I'm misunderstood & frustrated because these stupid fucking humans who 'take care' of me haven't learnt how to speak basic common Doglish yet. Idiots.

Anyway, thanks for letting me come and stay. I think Mammy Sharyn is off to hospital to have some liposuction done. She's really let herself go in the last few months and looks like a complete fat arse. How she thinks she'll ever fit into a size 10 again is beyond me. Daddy Alan is in hiding because he's MORTIFIED about the situation. I recently heard him on the phone to a mate saying he hadn't signed up for such a fat bird.

It was Christmas at the time so I can only assume that's when Mammy Sharyn started shoving food down her massive trap.

To be honest, I'm not entirely impressed with such unstable and dysfunctional masters, so if things work out between you and I, maybe we can hang out indefinitely. I'm sure my cousin Baxter will have something to say about that but honestly he can go and f*ck himself. All I ever want to do is wrap my paws around his indifferent, grimacing face, and all he wants to do is watch Will & Grace re-runs. I think, in time, he'll come around to my *way of thinking and be my best friend. Either that or I'm going to chew his pride-coloured lead to shreds while he's asleep. That'll learn him.*

My crazy, over-organised Mammy Sharyn has packed a bag for me that is RIDICULOUS, and not just because it's a knock-off Louis Vuitton monstrosity. She has my bowl in there (pink, how stereotypical), a red Kong that I usually eat peanut butter out of and that keeps me entertained for ages, and other toys and treats. Mostly, they don't give me treats unless I sit down and give them the paw. The pricks.

They also have their 'orders' that they like to shout at me, to get me to do things that make them feel better about themselves. So I can 'sit', 'lie down', 'give me the paw', 'go easy' when I'm a bit hyperactive, and Daddy Alan thinks it's great that I'll give him a 'high five', but mostly I'm just putting my paws up to say, 'Back the f*ck off asshole, would you?!'

My harness might look stupid, but it's because I get too choked with the lead going from my collar. I think I must have been beheaded in a past life – I'm thinking about talking to Psychic Sally about that. If you put the main bit around my neck, I can put my own paws through the side straps. Yes, I am that f*cking amazeballs.

So that's the low-down, Aunty Naomi. Everyone knows you're the coolest aunt, so there's no fear of my pissing on your floor. Promise. I will, however, require a LOT of affection, because they starve me of it here, and that's just tough shit for you. Get your cuddles on.

Lots of love and smelly poos,
Pearl xxxxxxxxxx

Chapter Six
LABOUR (MAY) DAY

Ass Monkey got us to the maternity hospital in approximately fourteen minutes flat, for a journey that should normally take about thirty-five.

I had a copy of the first Adele album in the CD player for precisely this journey that my pal Rory had burned for me. My plan was that she would calmly accompany us into the night so we might arrive to the maternity hospital in an Adele-induced romantic bubble.

In the end, we got to hear about three and a half songs in all, but at least they were all the good ones. To distract myself in between contractions, I roared along to 'Someone Like You' at the top of my lungs as Ass Monkey sped along the motorway and I texted my mates from the previous night's wedding, blaming their getting married before me for shocking me into labour.

So far, not the worst thing that ever happened and I thought to myself, 'This labour lark is kind of...*the craic*'.

When we bustled through the front doors of the hospital, the two twenty-something, 'got-shafted-with-the-poxy-nightshift' lads on reception could not have been less interested in my big news that **I was having a baby.**

'Sharyn Hayden, reporting for labour!' I roared at them gleefully, leaning against the reception desk with all the air of an expectant celebrity, whose imminent arrival might have been big news in the Dublin maternity hospital.

Evidently exhausted from the burden of gainful employment, neither chappie could manage a welcoming smile. Nor had they the energy to lift their wretched acne-filled heads up straight atop their little freckled necks to make eye contact.

'Just take a seat over there, love.'

One of them cocked his lifeless head in the general direction of the waiting area and got back to whatever amazing level he was on, on his PS3.

Em, where is the excitement, I wondered? Where is the handsome murse with my wheelchair to whisk me up to my private room that will be decorated by Willy Wonka (Lickable Labour Room Wallpaper anyone? Who needs gas and air when you can have pineapples that taste like pineapples?!)

The rest of the Adele album would be playing softly in the background of that private, candle-lit room, as Ass Monkey gently sprayed my face with the Evian face mist that every parenting website told me to buy.

And he would repeat over and over that he loves me so, so much and can't believe how lucky he is to have such a beautiful, calm, strong woman in his life to reproduce with.

Where was all that, eh? I ordered that version, didn't I?!

I sneakily checked out my fellow admittees in the waiting area – there were another three couples ahead of us, and everyone – besides me – seemed very calm. Ass Monkey and I shuffled over to take our own seats and we solemnly snuck in a few side glances at couples holding hands, serene pregnant women breathing very deeply and patiently and well, we were a bit embarrassed of ourselves to be honest.

Every time I had a contraction, the pain raged through my back and to be frank, gee area, so fiercely, that I had to stand up from my chair, turn to lean against the wall and Ass Monkey had to rub my back until the pain subsided (It was a reasonable request/order - depending on who you're talking to - that had been communicated the second the pains had begun that afternoon. Despite the fact that I do love to be rubbed, what the hell else was Ass Monkey supposed to be doing – just sitting there, staring at me? My painful undercarriage, he was!).

In any case I assumed that our pain, our highly energetic reactions to that pain, and our circumstances, being as different as they were to everyone else's in the room, meant that I was obviously further advanced in labour than they were.

I so concluded that we would be in need of some sort of urgent medical attention, please.

And as if that wasn't confirmation enough, the stopwatch on my iPhone read that my contractions were now coming every three and a half minutes! Shhiiite!

'Ask those lads what the fucking story is before I go behind that desk and deliberately break my waters all over their console screens,' I hissed.

(One does not like to be ignored, one doesn't, especially where the welfare of one's gee is concerned).

'Five minutes, they say,' Ass Monkey reported from the Back-To-Work-Scheme-manned-reception desk.

I started crying again. *Obviously.*

'Is it really sore, pet?' he enquired gently.

'No, it's not that,' I shook my head. 'I just don't think I'll survive the mortification if we have this baby in the lift. What will they say on Facebook?'

Agreeing that to have one's first child in between floors of a maternity hospital while the lift alarm rang non-stop in our ears would be the highest level of shite, Ass Monkey went back over again to Acne 1 and Acne 2 and begged. I'm fairly certain he also knew that if my prediction/fear came true, he would never hear the end of it for the rest of his natural born life and be blamed for not forcing those snotty-nosed brats to admit us.

Miraculously, the lot of us from the waiting area were sent up to be booked in soon after, and I am pleased to tell you that Jacob did not make any dramatic appearances during the ten-second two-story lift journey to their department.

We were greeted at admissions by a lovely young woman who took all our details, while I got up and down off my seat for the odd three-and-a-half-minutes-apart contraction here and there.

'Ok, Sharyn...' she began, '...wait, Hayden, are you related to any of the Haydens who worked here by any chance? Like, Shane Hayden?'
  'Ah yes,' I forced a smile, 'Shane is my brother.'

It's probably important to note at this point, that I have had family working in the maternity hospital we attended. All three of my brothers have worked there at one point or another, starting as 'visual technicians' (window washers) when they were on holidays from school, and then two of them worked as engineers there when they qualified from college.
  My dad also worked in the accounts department at the time so needless to say, I had been well looked after in all of my appointments and any contact I had with the hospital in general. Of course, I'm sure everyone else gets well taken care of too, but hands up who else was greeted with 'Here she is! Let's get the air fanned out for her!' by the hilarious head of the semi-private clinic? Hmmm? Didn't think so...

Anyhoo, back to the admissions office and the 'inquisitive' girl checking us in. I had just confirmed that yes, I was Sharyn Hayden, sister to the Shane that used to work there too. So what?

A look crossed her face – a look I have been around the block enough times to know what the jaysus it meant. It was a bit, you know, fluttery. A bit *flushed*.

'Isn't that gas?' she mused, nervously re-arranging items on her desk that needed no re-arranging. She was clearly trying to keep her shit together but this wonky gooey smile that was transfixed to her face gave her away entirely.
'I remember it so well when he worked here. He was such lovely guy, Shane. Em, and how is he?'

I immediately fixed my gaze at a point on the wall over her head, whilst simultaneously trying not to see any bit of Ass Monkey's face in my peripheral vision.
Because I knew, *I knew*, that if we locked eyes, my face would contort into that of horrified about-to-puke-coz-someone-fancies-my-brother face. It's the same one I pull when watching *I'm A Celebrity, Get Me Out Of Here!* (PS What is WRONG with those people?!)
Was this really happening, I wondered? Was I actually going to have to endure a giddy girl fawning over one of my brothers while I had contractions right in front of her face?

'Married,' I told her, no beating around the bush. 'One baby, very happy. What a wonderful coincidence that you know him. Where do we go now please?'

Gooey face discarded, Admissions Chick directed us down to the 'other' admissions (who can say why) with a wave and a weak call of 'Tell Shane I was asking for him!' No, surprisingly not 'Best of luck with your labour!' or anything helpful like that, just a message of desperate hope to my bro.

When we finally got to our labour room to wait for the midwife, Ass Monkey and I got busy organising ourselves and our luggage for what was coming.

Clothes off, nightdress on, jewellery off, face spritz and lip balm at the ready. iPod for the dock that I was so sure they would provide so I could have the musical soundtrack of my choice for the birth of my baby.

I was of course armed with the ever-important 'Birthing Plan', printed out, filled in and laminated for good measure. Throughout my pregnancy, I had envisaged myself as a bit a 'Mother Earth' about the whole thing. I hoped to breastfeed for as long as possible, I wanted a drug-free birth; I had even investigated the possibility of having a water birth at the house.

(That plan was ultimately only scuppered by the realisation that if someone called in to offer any amazing 'advice' in the middle of it all – then I would have to drown them in said birthing pool and growing up in prison was not the start I wanted for my child).

I was determined to remain all natural, all at one with my body, all woman.

'I'd like the epidural, please,' I announced to the very first midwife who walked in the door.

Ass Monkey snuffled out a guffaw. Out with that one sentence went every single painful conversation about 'my body is built for having babies, you know, and drugs will just interfere with the whole beautiful, natural process' that he had to pretend to be interested in for the previous nine months.

The midwife smiled and told me I was about to be examined. I'm not going to lie to you: of all the things I've had up my vagina in my time, that midwife's hand was beyond a shadow of a doubt the worst. Very harsh, very unwelcome, very unkind. I concluded that there was no way she could be a lesbian, not now, not ever.

'You can't have an epidural,' she explained matter-of-factly.

'Oh no! Why? Is it too late?'

I dramatically grasped for Ass Monkey's hand on one side, clutched my nightdress at the neckline with the other, terrified for us both.

We held our breaths, staring at her, waiting for the inevitable news that our baby was about to be delivered in the next three minutes and that we should brace ourselves for the onslaught of press interest into 'The Quickest Labour On Record' that the hospital had ever seen.

'No, quite the opposite, Miss Hayden' she sighed. 'I'm afraid you're not actually in labour at all.'

Chapter Seven
ANGRY BIRD

Ass Monkey and I were sent packing off to the labour ward, to wait for my actual labour to kick in.

This next bit of information won't be wholly scientific, but apparently what was going on was that I was in pre-labour and my cervix hadn't started to open up yet. Pre-labour. I didn't remember anyone, in any of all the feckin' antenatal classes I went to, talking about pre-labour. I. Was. Mortified.

Furthermore, if I was freaking out about the pains I was having during 'Pre-labour', then what the actual fuck would I be like when the proper contractions started?

Ass Monkey and I settled in to our little cubby that had a hospital curtain drawn for privacy and tried to distract ourselves from the moaning and groaning coming from The Valley Of The Damned outside.

We did the only thing we knew we could do well in that moment in time: we started playing Angry Birds.

Keeping one eye on his phone's stopwatch, Ass Monkey would give me a ten-second heads up that another blasting contraction was on the way. He dressed it up very nicely:

'Step away from the iPad, young lady,' he'd inform me. 'You've got a back massage coming up.'

Like the good little massage junkie that I am, I would fire my last birdie-missile at the unsuspecting piggies in space and brace myself. When we completed each 'massage', we had a high five. Coz that's just the way we nut jobs roll.

After another an hour or so, I was examined again and this time my waters broke in response. Nothing like another hand shovelled up there to get things moving, if you ask me.

And for whatever reason, the hospital staff decided that this was the most opportune moment to,

A) Get me to walk down the corridor to go back into the delivery room ('Mop On Aisle Four!') and,
B) Have us sit back down at the weird second re-admissions place to hand over our details again. * FACE PALM *

I was struggling at that point, no longer feeling like chatting (or high-fiving, or angry-birding) and a little bit humiliated that there was a trail of my insides now visible up and down the hospital corridor.

As my body was lifted off the seat once more by another contraction, I eyeballed Ass Monkey and a voice, not my own, but akin to a Dot

Cotton/Twink/Smoking forty Johnny Blues-A-Day combo, emanated from me:

'I want that fucking epidural. Do you hear me? Now.' We got back into our labour room. A brand new midwife greeted me. Great.

'Hop up on the bed there now, Sharyn, and we'll have a look at you,' she smiled.

I stopped in my demented tracks at the door. I looked at her, I looked at the bed, I felt my damp nightdress sticking to me and I didn't take another step. Ass Monkey looked confused, wondering if was I about to change my mind and make a run for it.

'I would like the epidural please,' I replied, super-maternity-glued to the spot.

Hadn't I asked about this a few hours ago and yet no one had yet acknowledged it nor reassured me that it was coming? What was the problem?

'Well now, we'll have to examine you,' the midwife smiled again. 'You might not be able to get it now, you understand.'

It is Ass Monkey's recollection that I nearly pulled this poor lady's head off in response, but I don't remember it that way. I remember my mind flitting back to the faces of the nurses and midwives that I did ask for the epidural, who hadn't delivered it, and planning on pulling *their* heads off.

On top of that, I also remember thinking, 'I'm in shitloads of pain right now, this midwife is a medical professional – is that the most comforting thing she could have said to me right now? How about a 'No problem honey, just hop up on the bed there and we'll take a quick look at you', or an 'Epidural? I happen to have one right here in my back pocket, where do you want it?' Or the best announcement one could receive in this kind of moment, 'The anesthetist is on the way and you're at the top of her list, Ms. Hayden.'

I do have to agree with Ass Monkey here. I may not have 'pulled her head off', but I wasn't exactly nice either. I was pissed off – I was tired, sore, definitely scared, had had hands rooting around inside me on and off for hours, was a bit scarlet over losing control of my bodily functions and fluids and all I wanted was for someone to be nice to me.

I have accepted the odd fob-off in my time but on this particular undercarriage-is-on-fire day, I wasn't having it. Having vowed not to pull out the 'My family works here' card until met with an absolute emergency, I felt that this, here and now, was definitely an S.O.S. situation.

'I. Have. Been. Asking. For. An. Epidural. Since. I. Came. In,' I hissed (My head possibly turned 360 degrees on my neck right there. There was also possible fire flaring from my nostrils/earlobes).
'I. Will. Not. Be. Getting. Into. The. Bed. Until. You. Call. The. Anesthetist.'

Ass Monkey relayed to me (a lot) later that he had been feeling sorry for me up until that point, but then, he felt sorry for *her*.

I was momentarily stopped in the middle of my protest by another contraction and yes, more mess on the floor, so I *completely* lost my shit and any manners that went with it.

'My dad works here. Maybe you know him, Tommy from (*coughs*) Accounts?'

Eventually, I was persuaded to get up on to the bed to be examined and it was agreed that an epidural could, in fact, be administered and so the anesthetist was called. Thank fuck.

Of course, there was karmic punishment for being such an asshole to the nurse. The epidural needle had to be inserted a little higher up my spine than the anesthetist would have liked, because of the ridiculous 'tramp stamp' tattoo I have on my back.

I had been fairly regretful for some time in my thirties of the 'Chinese symbol for Taurus' that was right above my arse, but never more so than on this day. Tattoos are always a great idea at the time, kids ;o)

But blissful painless peace took over once the drugs had kicked in! I told the anesthetist that I was actually in love with her; I returned to my high-fiving, smiling self and even had a little snooze.

(I am pained to report that Ass Monkey didn't though – he mentioned that he found the side of the bed 'extremely uncomfortable' and 'impossible' to get any sleep on. Yes, he seriously did. He's still alive, don't worry, has just suffered a dead arm for his troubles. Both arms, naturally.)

All in all, my little 'tingles' had started at lunchtime on Sunday. We got to the hospital and were admitted just before midnight. And at 6 a.m. the following morning, I was ready to deliver. Not bad going at all.

I had THE COOLEST midwife in the world EVER, to help deliver Jacob. She was from Cork and had a cheerleading chant that I can only describe as being akin to The Tongue Twisters from the kid's show Bosco back in the day. If you remember, at the end of every chant, they took a breath, their necks elongated and their voices went higher? This chick could have invented them.

'Poosh, poosh, poosh, poosh, POOSH, POOSH, POOSH, POOOOSHHHHHH!'
'Keep going, keep going, keep going, don't stop, DON'T STOP, DONNNNN'T STOPP!'
'You're doing great, you're doing great, you're doing great, you're DOING GREATT!'
'Poosh, poosh, poosh, poosh, POOSH, POOSH, POOOSH, POOOOOOOOSSSSSHHH!'

I loved her. I sent her a thank you card and gift afterwards, but it will never be enough. I think she should be recorded, bottled, re-sold and earn millions, because she's a legend.

So just before 7 a.m., Ass Monkey and I had the biggest high five of all as Jacob made his way into the world, to a rapturous chorus of Cork-accented cheering and Ass Monkey's polite enquiries of 'Does he have red hair? What colour hair does he have? Is it red? Is he ginger?' (Have I mentioned that I'm an original redhead and PROUD OF IT? Ass Monkey doesn't necessarily feel the same way).

High as a kite on epidural drugs, gas and air, pethidine and pure euphoria, I proceeded to inform everyone in the room how much I loved them all over again.

A young trainee nurse came in and hugged us both congratulations – it was the sweetest thing. My brother Eoghan, about to start work, stuck his head in to share in all the joy. I tried really hard to cry but I was *way* too high.

We got Eoghan to take our very first family pic: Ass Monkey looking wrecked because the poor thing didn't have anywhere comfortable to sleep, me looking red in the face but with false eyelashes from the wedding perfectly intact and this little perfect bundle between us. It was the bomb.

And I'll let you in on a little secret: no matter how tough you think you are, no matter where you're from, the prospect and process of giving birth to another human being is an extremely daunting one that should never be taken lightly.

Personally? I shit myself.

Chapter Eight
MAMMY GOES WALKIES

In July 2010, I got my own way for probably the first time in my relationship with Ass Monkey when we he finally gave in to my pestering him about getting a dog. Pearl was eight weeks old when we picked her up, and her terrified, palm-sized self shook and shook as I held her to my chest all the way in the car. Thankfully, she had the decency not to shit or wee on me – she was a lady from the start.

The first couple of weeks with her were not unlike having a newborn in the house. We woke to her cries during the night and would go to her little bed in the sitting room, lift her out, hold and soothe her until she went back to sleep again. I productively used this extra awake time to re-watch *Will & Grace* from start to finish (as if I needed an excuse).

Once, during a particularly funny episode where Jack mistakes the real Cher for a drag Queen impersonator, Pearl placed her tiny paw on my arm and let out a contented sigh in her sleep, communicating (I believed) that she trusted me and accepted me as her new mammy.

I am not ashamed to admit that this tiny gesture moved me so much that I bawled my head off and whisper-promised into her little fluffy ear that I would look after her forever. As if she understood what I was saying - which is stupid from both a 'she was only eight weeks old' perspective and the fact that she's a *dog*. **I know.**

By the following January, I was pregnant and Pearl was a great source of help and comfort to me. She kept me active by demanding to be walked around the great big football fields by our home and when I rested on the couch or in bed, she snuggled right in beside the bump – warming me and keeping a protective guard over our little growing family.

Aside from all the unwanted baby and parenting advice and questions from people both whom I did and didn't know, they almost always brought up the subject of our dog and asked, 'What are you going to do about Pearl?'

At first, I used to stutter and blubber through my answers, 'Oh we're just going to keep a very close eye on her with the baby, she's very kind natured, it'll be fine,' etc. But eventually I started getting pissed off. What did that mean, what was I going to 'do' about her? She was a tiny white puppy for Christ's sake – not, for example, a *pedophile*.

Eventually, just out of devilment, I used to look these interrogators in the eye and sincerely reply, 'As soon as the baby comes along, we're just going to get the shovel out of the shed and put her down ourselves. Thanks so much for asking.'

At the end of our first week at home with newborn Jacob, Ass Monkey's fab sister Naomi returned Pearl back from her 'holidays'. She had kindly offered to take her for longer but my hormones wouldn't hear of it and I demanded her return (In hindsight, it would have been no harm to have her go on a two-weeker. Or a one-monther. But I only say that now that the pair of them, baby and dog combined, drive me bat-shit crazy on a daily basis).

After her initial suspicion and distaste towards me, which is always the case when I 'abandon' her for any amount of time, Pearl eventually came to me for a cuddle. I lifted her up to see and sniff little Jacob in his Moses basket and she wagged her tail straight away. Phew, we all sighed – so she doesn't seem to want to eat his face after all.

Twenty minutes later, she was scratching at the front door. *Walkies*. Twenty minutes after that, I figured out how to assemble the pram, put the baby in it, find my runners and get us all out the door. If I walked for two and a half minutes that day, I was very lucky. My body wasn't quite able for it yet and at that point, I really wasn't sure that my vagina would ever speak to me again. But every day, Pearl stood at that door, and demanded to be walked. So out we went.

If I didn't feel like it, if had spent two hours crying because I was exhausted and felt overwhelmed from New Motherhood, if the house was upside down, my leggings were on inside out and the washing machine had leaked all over the kitchen floor – Pearl got walked.

And that meant that I got walked, and Jacob got walked. We all got out of the house every day, come hell or high water.

When I think about it now and my emotional state generally at the time, I think Pearl saved me in a way. I had suffered with mild depression here and there over the years and really anticipated that it might kick in again after the baby was born. But it didn't happen.

That's not to say that I didn't have miserable days. That's not to say that I wasn't narky for about a year and a half. But I thankfully didn't suffer from any form of serious post-natal depression that we hear about and hope to avoid.

All of those walks helped me to eventually lose the baby weight, forced some fresh air into my lungs, got me away from the trudge of working from home and noticing all those dirty corners that you imagine need cleaning (They don't, by the way. Take. A. Nap).

We of *course* watched Pearl very closely when she was around Jacob, particularly when he started crawling because she was so freaked out! That was her space, that floor, and suddenly this other tiny little being was invading it.

Every time she grumbled or growled at him, she got put outside into the garden and told NO. Eventually, she worked out that growling wasn't allowed because she's a clever little thing and stopped doing it.

And although I still refer to Pearl as my 'first child', I will now take a big, deep breath and reluctantly admit this: **Babies Are More Important Than Puppies**.

There, I said it. Please don't judge me, dog lovers. Be assured: Pearl is still treated like royalty in our house, and gets snuck into the bed beside me at every opportunity. ;o)

Anyway, as kids get older, the emphasis on whom is potentially more harmful to who changes. These days, I mostly try to keep toddler Jacob away from Pearl, so that he doesn't pull her tail/feed her chocolate/shove his toy cars up her arse.

Generally speaking, they totally love each other and Jacob calls her his 'best friend'…

…which is both heart-warming and just a little bit Mowgli from *The Jungle Book* all in one.

Chapter Nine
BOOB, INTERRUPTED

The few days after giving birth to Jacob in the hospital will always be a bit of a blur to me. All of the drugs – from the epidural to the painkillers I then was topped up with – kept me in La-La Land for about a week. My parents arrived, flowers and cards arrived, Eoghan and his partner Nicola arrived, nurses, midwives, consultants from the hospital who knew my dad and Eoghan and who wanted to say hello arrived – it was a really busy time.

I recall one day where I tried to brush my teeth three times over the space of one hour and a half, and every time I got the toothpaste onto the brush and just had it at my mouth, there was another knock on the door.

Not that I'm complaining. In fairness, when everyone had left for the day, when Ass Monkey was sent home and it was just me and this little fella in the cot beside me, who woke me up with his cries during the night, I hadn't a clue what I was supposed to do. Not an iota. And I wished that everyone would come back so I wouldn't be left to be the only one responsible for him.

Although I had planned for Jacob and carried him and read up on all the literature I could on what life would be like when he came along, and what I would need to do to look after him – I was still monumentally surprised at his presence! I remember being really confused as to what these little cries were that invaded my dreams.

When I'd eventually wake up properly and focus in on this little boy body writhing and crying out beside me, I didn't know what to do with him! What did he want? Was he unhappy? Did he need to be fed *again?* Why couldn't he be a twelve-hours-a-night-sleeper like his mother?

Despite every baby & parenting professional I had met during the course of my pregnancy telling me that breast feeding was the way forward (I did ask once, in an ante-natal class, whether or not we should bring bottles in with us to the hospital, you know, in case the breastfeeding didn't work out for everyone? Blanked.com. Seriously.) – anyway, despite all of that, Jacob had an agenda of his own and was born into the world decidedly anti-breastfeeding.

Akin to my hippy, (misguided) Mother Earth ideals of having a drug-free water birth at home, I had this other idea that I would have absolutely zero problem breastfeeding.

I convinced myself that my baby and I would be as one, it would come really naturally to me and it would be this glorious, beautiful thing that would nourish him and bond us together forever.

I was determined not to give a shite about feeding him in public either, if he needed it, and had bought a couple of those maternity tops that give your baby easy access to your boob so that you don't have to strip down to your waist in the middle of an Eddie Rockets diner.

In fact, I was *so* sure that I would be breastfeeding that I didn't even buy a bottle sterilizer! We spent €10 on a travel steriliser and that was it. Boobie all the way, we declared. Or so we thought.

Jacob latched on ok at the hospital at first, but then would fall asleep almost immediately into feeding and so we knew he wasn't getting enough. A night nurse did attempt to 'help' me by essentially assaulting my boob and ramming it into his mouth, but that approach didn't work either (what a surprise).

Eventually, Ass Monkey took a close look at him and thought that Jacob was maybe a bit jaundiced. I mean, he was very tanned, but I had vainly hoped that was just a nod to Ass Monkey's sallow skin, and our little man was going to be a little on the mochaccino side (Score!).

A quick visit to the nurse's desk to voice his concern and Ass Monkey was shooed away with a flick of the hand, assured that our baby was 'fine'.

Twenty-four hours later, Jacob was under the lamps in the ICU unit, with a teeny tiny eye mask on. As it turns out, his daddy's instinct was right on and he *was* jaundiced. We should have insisted on a test when Ass Monkey thought there was something wrong, and didn't. I've since decided that even if you think you're clueless because you're new to parenthood, there can be no medical substitute for your own instinct, so don't take no – or nursey wrist-flickage - for an answer.

We did assert ourselves from then on. By the end of the week, opinions differed as to whether we should be sent home, or if Jacob should stay in the ICU another while, so we insisted that he stay. Yes it cost us more money, but we knew that was incidental to the little man's health. Plus, I was petrified to go home with him in case anything happened.

While Jacob got his suntan on in an incubator, Ass Monkey and I left the comforts of the hospital and checked in to a nearby hotel and then…then…the drugs completely wore off and the 'Baby Blues' kicked in. Oh by Jesus did they kick in.

I was exhausted, sore in my sorest places, my boobs were shunned, my fake eyelashes had well and truly fallen out - apart from those weird stubborn ones in the middle of your eyelid that refuse to go anywhere - and Jacob wasn't with me to make it all worthwhile. I bawled my head off as poor Ass Monkey lay awake in the bed beside me and despaired, not having a clue what to do.

We dropped down to the hospital every three hours to feed him. I had been gifted a loan of a breast pump from the hospital and by the reaction from the nurses when I delivered a full bottle of milk after each pumping session, my boobs were finally making themselves useful.

'Is that all yours?' they'd ask, incredulous, as I dropped another bottle down to the fridge.

'Er, yes?' I'd reply nervously (I mean, was I being accused of breast milk theft? Who does that?). 'Is that, em, good?'

'Sure that'll keep him going for three feeds!' they'd exclaim joyously.

Finally! My tiny boobies were good for something! So even though the staff had enough to keep Jacob going through the night, I wanted to see him and feed him myself. I dragged Ass Monkey and I out of the warm hotel bed at regular intervals during the night and up to the hospital to stare at this little tiny body under the 'sun lamps'.

He honestly didn't look too unlike someone who was really enjoying himself. At one point, he actually even had his little hands resting up around the back of his head. I was only short of sticking a martini in there and a lei around his neck.

We were thankfully sent home the next day at noon, and we couldn't get there fast enough - except that we had forgotten to practise fixing the stupid baby car seat into the back seat of the car and had zero idea how to do it.

Baby Jacob and I spent twenty minutes waiting on the side of the road while Eoghan and Ass Monkey (both engineers, may I add!), tried to figure it out. FYI that's one of those things you're supposed to practise over and over before the baby arrives. As usual, we skipped this very important bit, thinking, 'How hard can it possibly be?'

Idiots.

Home, at last, home. We got into our PJs and dressing gowns and cracked open the champagne. WE DID IT! Jacob's jaundice tests were clear, he was hungry enough to feed and so the boobies were out again. It wasn't the natural process I thought it would be, but I persevered. And Ass Monkey and I delighted in the size of my knockers and it isn't every day I can say that.

We enjoyed a peaceful night of just us; our new little family, looking at each other, smiling gooily in disbelief that we had this little person snoozing between us and we were super loved up like never before.

As of 9am the very next day…the visitors came. And they came in droves. It was mostly our own fault because we were so hyper excited that we *told* them to come. But that meant we had to clean up, wash ourselves, put the kettle on, get the biccies in and really fucked ourselves in the head with the pressure of it all.

But there were others…who we didn't invite, who we weren't expecting, who knocked on the door just the second we had gotten the baby to sleep and were planning on a nap of our own, or the second I had decided on a topless breastfeeding session (you know, the ones with just your knickers on and your dressing gown flung open – because you aren't expecting anyone).

Eventually, I stationed my mother in the sitting room to act as security, and whenever it looked like someone was planning on settling in for the long haul, or I was getting tired, she would run them.

My mam is great like that: she's a polite, well-brought up south-side Dublin lady through and through, so when she takes a moment to say something in a serious tone like, 'It's been *so* nice to see you,' with those steely blue eyes of hers, you get the message that it's time to hit the road.

Based on our unforgettable experiences during those first few visitor-heavy weeks, here is an extensive list of those who should and those who should not, visit in the first few weeks after a new baby is born. Feel free to make a sticker out of it and staple it to your front door.

Those Who Should Visit:

1.   Grandparents. As much as they like. The bond that grandkids and grandparents have is so frickin' cool.

2.   The postman. Only as far as the front door obviously, with cards and pressies and with any luck, a reassuring smile for you in your wrecked, undressed state that he isn't judging you. We had the coolest postman who would sometimes leave a note saying, 'Have a parcel for you. Will try again tomorrow. Hope I didn't wake you'. Loved him!

3.   Any person who is *invited*, but those people need to follow a certain baby-visiting etiquette which includes:

A)   Being on time. Your time of visit is probably scheduled around naps, feeding, visits to the public health nurse, deep-seated desires to spend ten minutes alone - and,

B)   Fecking off home after a maximum of one hour.

(I am guilty of often being crap at this one to other friends with kids, staying too long talking shite so, sorry mates. Just tell me to shut up and leave, will you?!).

4.   Anyone who is a dab hand at the dishes/window washing/fixing the leak & suspicious smell from the bathroom cabinet.

5.   Those who would like to walk the dog OR bring any other kids in the house out for a walk/on a play date/to their own house overnight.

6.   Helpful, considerate people who have brought vast quantities food and don't plan on eating it themselves.

Those Who Should Stay Away:

1.   The uninvited and the unexpected. Why anyone would show up on a doorstep on spec, never mind that of a new parent, is so completely beyond me. And why they would ALSO then stay for more than two hours is just psychotic.

2.   Those who are emotionally unstable and wish to talk about their own problems for an extended period of time. Just suck up your issues with your mother who abandoned you for a better life in Australia for this ONE HOUR, smile and coo and ask that parent how THEY are. Discuss this and this only. Please and thank you.

3.   Those who have no concept of **not** ringing the doorbell repeatedly. What happens in your brain exactly? Do you think 'Oh here's Sharyn's house. She's just had a baby. I bet the baby isn't asleep and loves the sound of the doorbell. Here, let me try it. Wait, they're not answering? They must be inside there, frozen with excitement that the bell might ring again and that's why she hasn't opened the door yet. Maybe I'll just place my finger on the button here and never take it off. They'll love that'.
THIS IS NOT NORMAL BEHAVIOUR, YOU TOTAL WEIRDO FACE.

4. The parents of your partner's ex-girlfriend.

What. The. Actual. Fuck.

Chapter Ten
RAGE AGAINST THE BABY MACHINE

Ass Monkey and I somehow managed to buy the most ridiculous buggy that was ever invented. It was one of those 'All In' travel systems, meaning that the pram bit was also the car seat that could be removed from the buggy frame and fixed to the back seat of the car when needed.

It also meant that when Jacob was big enough, the pram bit could be put away, and, with the assistance of a few hundred YouTube tutorials and five degrees in engineering, one could eventually figure out how to put the other bits together to make it a 'Big Boy Buggy'. The hood of it also played music when you hit a particular button. We thought it was kind of amazing.

'It'll last you for years,' the young one said in The Buggy Shop. 'I'd say three years in annyways.'

I did some major damage to a back muscle the first time I lifted Jacob in the car seat bit, the few yards from the car into my parent's house. He weighed nothing, but the stupid car seat/pram bit could have been made from lead.

I was barely even able to fit the whole thing through the front door of the apartment! Between dragging Pearl back out of the way, so that she wouldn't get trampled on by the gigantic buggy wheels, and operating a 64-point turn, just getting to the foot path outside was an exhausting ordeal in itself.

It took both my mam and I to carry Jacob in the car seat to the hospital for a check-up one day, each of us taking a side and hauling him in the doors like a big basket of laundry. Even with her help, it was still unbelievably heavy.

At visits to the supermarket, I knocked things off shelves up and down every aisle, bending my already wrecked back, up and down, up and down, picking up tins of beans and boxes of Ready Brek.

We had been duped! Mesmerised by its shiny red exterior and music-playing hood, we assumed an air of parental 'coolness' because we would be providing our kid with a built-in sound track while he got shoved around the streets of North County Dublin. We had been gifted some cash towards buying it from one of my brothers, Noel (Jacob's now godfather – always pick the ones with the cash) and we went to town on it.

Our thinking was 'If we have the money, we should spend it on something really special'. Practicality? Ease of use? Don't be ridiculous, those concerns never even entered our heads. The buggy LOOKED AWESOME.

Eventually, I borrowed a car seat from a friend - a regular one. It was so light – even with Jacob in it – that I could literally carry it over my head with a straight arm and no wobbles. I nearly cried with relief and was converted forever.

Aside from the buggy being a bit ridiculous in size and shape, my adjustment from an independent, free-spirited woman to a buggy-pushing mammy came with its very own set of logistical complications. To be honest, I initially found the whole thing incredibly frustrating in general.

For example, take the following scenario. No, let's call it a pop quiz. Ready? Ok, on your stretch marks...

You are walking to the supermarket from home with your baby in his buggy and dog in tow. Your dog is so allergic to the notion of being tied up by the trolley bay while you shop, that she deliberately slips right out of her collar and lead, and runs away from you in the direction of a busy road of traffic...

Do you:

A) Ignore said dog for the drama queen that she is, presume she'll find her way home when she's hungry and carry on into the shops.
B) Turn the extraordinarily heavy buggy around and run after said dog, pushing said buggy, with semi-broken vagina, sore back and sore boob bits in case the dog gets flattened by a truck.

C) Stare after said dog in shock and dismay, and hope that the six or eight people who she is running past might take a minute out of their really busy lives to grab her for you.

D) Slam the breaks on the buggy by the trolley bay, and run after said dog like a mad woman, screaming 'SIT! SIT!' (past the six or eight people who are still doing nothing to help, FFS), whilst simultaneously glancing back to buggy repeatedly, shitting oneself that someone might rob it. And then calmly realise that no one would be able to budge the fucking thing anyway.

'D' was the answer on this particular day. By some miracle, Pearl actually did sit – she eventually took my hysterical tone seriously, I guess – so I carried her back to the buggy, put her lead back on and we all went straight home without a single solitary item on the shopping list.

I never again attempted walking to the shops with both of them in tow after that day.

Having only ever lived in the world as a single, child-free person, there were many other fantastic eye openers that I discovered along the way as a new parent.

For starters, I could no longer walk freely up escalators in shopping centres. I now had to queue for an age at the lifts as four buggies got out, one tried to get in, no one held the doors and whoosh! off the lift went to another floor as we all waited for another ten minutes.

I also discovered that if I left the house without any sort of essential item such as a soother, a change of clothes, a pre-made bottle or – God forbid – a nappy or two, then an actual general state of emergency would ensue. I will place bets for hard cash with everyone that whatever that item is that you have left behind on the kitchen counter – will be the exact item in demand on your journey.

Not only are you guaranteed that your child will wail for the soother, piss or shit through his clothes, and wail again with hunger - you are also 100% guaranteed that the feelings of self-hatred, guilt and stress will overtake you and keep you in their grasp for a couple of days afterwards at the very least.

Oh, and not only that, but you'll have to spend extra money you don't have on more of this stuff that you have sitting idle at home. Disaster zone.

I've done it, several times over. Every time I've left without a change of clothes, Jacob has had an arse explosion only superseded by that scene in *Bridesmaids*.

Once, in the Arnotts department store in Dublin city, Jacob destroyed himself with so much of his own shit that I had to wrap him in paper hand towels from the bathroom until I could buy him a new (crazy expensive) babygro.

Ultimately, I wheeled a semi-naked baby around a public shopping centre in a buggy for half an hour, who was wearing nothing but a nappy, a pair of socks, and patches of soggy, torn-and-ready-to-disintegrate blue hand paper to hide his modesty. I am convinced that the other shoppers must have deduced for at least a millisecond that I had stolen the child and contemplated calling security.

I also had no idea that most supermarkets have trollies that are actually designed for mammies with small kids. No clue! Until it was too late to be considered useful information, I used to shove Jacob, car seat and all, into the body of the trolley and just stuff all the groceries around his happy head.

How was I to know that there were special ones that you could clip the car seat into? I never had any need for them before so I hadn't noticed them. But seriously, how genius is that?!

And when Jacob got a little bigger, there were reclining seats on top of the trolleys for His Lordship's comfort. And if you had twins – two reclining seats, side by side. Astonishing!

Did you also know that there are specific toilets almost everywhere for mammies with kids to go to, to feed or change them? I didn't. Up until Jacob was about eight months old, I used to charge the pair of us to the farthest wall at the end of the cubicles in the ladies toilet, and park the buggy there.

Then I'd fling myself onto the toilet with one foot keeping the door almost closed, doubling myself over to one side to make sure the buggy was still there, or craning my neck to see that the wheels were static under the door.

What did I think was going to happen? That if I did see them move, my bare arse and I would run out through to the main shopping mall in the Pavilions in Swords, screaming 'Give me back my bayyyybeeeee!'? (Sorry, I know, I have imagined it too, and it's not pretty, is it? When you picture it for yourself, do me the courtesy of at least having me cover my crotch area with both hands, would you? Thanks loads).

No need for all this kerfuffle, parents, there are very nice and spacious family-friendly toilets, where not only is there room inside for you and your buggy (if it's a normal-sized one), but you can change your baby's bum on a nice waist-high changing table to save your back, and there's a toilet for you too. It's a miracle!

It also seriously prevents you from having an awkward 'Baby Monitoring Wee Accident' during the other 'method', which basically involves you pissing down your own leg and into your socks a little bit.

Unaccustomed as I am to shopping at the upmarket Dundrum Shopping Centre on Dublin's south side – I'm more of a Jervis Street Shopping Centre kind of gal, me – I did find myself in the public toilets there one time.

For those of you who have never frequented La Dundrum S.C, let me just paint a picture for you. The 'public toilets' there are not like those you might desperately stumble into for an emergency wee at, say, Pearse Street train station in Dublin city. The kind of toilets, you know, where you are greeted with an ultra-violet, junkie-thwarting lighting situation (which is not conducive to inserting a tampon, FYI).

Nor are the toilets in Dundrum akin to any you might find at, say, a music festival. The best example of their condition comes from the mouth of Ass Monkey himself, when we visited the inaugural No Place Like Dome festival a few years back.

The Portaloo-To-Festival-Reveller quota was way off, in the 'Are there seriously only FOUR of them?!' category, resulting in our discovering several 'presents' lined up beside our jeep the morning after the revelry.

Whilst yours truly refused to exit said jeep until we had not only left the campsite, but also shoved the jeep through the most bad ass car wash we could find several times over, Ass Monkey bravely made a dash for the main arena for coffee.

As he passed the portaloos, holding his breath, he could hear a voice calling out from inside one of the units. It was girl crying out to her hysterical and unsympathetic friends outside:

'Oh my God, oh my Godddddd it's disguuusssting….
Oh…oh fuck…oh no….
Girls, I'm after puking all ovvvverrr myyyysellllfffff…!'

No, no, no. The 'public toilets' in Dundrum S.C. are pristine, designed to the flash level that one would expect and never run out of toilet paper.

It's like weeing at a 5-star hotel, with the exact same quotient of richer-than-you, thinner-than-you, scorpier-than-you clientele present. It was at said jacks that I spotted A Brand New Mammy.

Before I became a mammy myself, I would never have noticed this woman in a million years. I would have been gossiping with my own mammy (my shopping partner of choice), checking myself out in the mirror, wishing for bigger boobs, a straighter nose and an end to eyebrow psoriasis...completely oblivious to anyone else around really, never mind a struggling parent.

But now that I am a mammy, I notice other women with babies, or who are pregnant, all the time. This woman, in the Dundrum S.C. toilets, had a tiny new baby in a pram and was nervously looking at the toilet stalls, back to her new sleeping baby, to the stalls again – over and over and over.

She had the look of a nervous, confused, twitchy person and in a second, I knew what great impossibility she was contemplating.

'Need to pee?' I asked gently.

My newfound wisdom as a fellow wet-behind-the-ears parent had somewhat turned me into a mother-saving Oprah-esque type. But infinitely paler, obviously.

'How...how do you do it...?' she trailed off, completely perplexed by the logistics. I didn't blame her.

'I'll mind the baby and you go ahead,' I instructed.

Without batting an eyelid, she and her ready-to-burst bladder ran straight into a cubicle. I mean, I could have been anyone, but apparently I have an honest face AND my mam by my side does lend me some credibility. I mean, she was born a southsider after all, you know. Yar and double forking yar.

When New Mammy got back to us and thanked us, I let her in on my running the buggy down to the cubicle at the end technique and told her, with a nod and a wink and a pat on her back, that she could now take that little gem with her for the rest of her journey into motherhood.

'Or,' as my increasingly smart-arsed own mother pointed out, 'there's always the baby changing facilities next door. They usually have a toilet in them for the parents too.'

Ahem.

Eventually, Ass Monkey and I got rid of our crazy 'travel system' buggy. We were booked on a flight to Leeds to celebrate my nephews' birthday and christening (a 2-in-1 – great idea), and realised that there was no way on God's great earth that Ryanair were going to consider our stupid buggy as 'standard' and let us on board without charging us the entire cost to hire a separate plane to get it to the UK.

So off popped Ass Monkey to Argos, where he promptly purchased the easiest, lightest, slimmest, most co-operative buggy that ever existed, for the grand sum of €50.

Not only did the Ryanair staff pop it through for us without any fuss, but they also gave Jacob the coolest welcome ever for his first time on an airplane, shaking his tiny hand and posing with him for photos.

I'm not one to normally say this but, Best. Ryanair. Flight. Ever.

Chapter Eleven
BAPTISM BY SMOKING

Ass Monkey and I don't know what we are. I mean, we know we're people, human beings and everything – *we're not Scientologists FFS* - we know that we're Dubs, north-side Dubs to be more specific. We know that we are our parents' children and we know that we are business people and we know that we are brother and sister – no, not to each other, you weirdo - to our **siblings.**

We know that we are students of the world, that we're alright looking, that he's an amazing cook and that I have two dishes I can get away with. We know that we are caretakers to one little dog and one little boy-child. We also know that sometimes, we can be a pair of assholes to be around. Who isn't.

But all of this means nothing in the country we live in. In Ireland, the goodness of your heart, the conviction of your actions, the area you grew up in or how much money is or isn't in the bank is 100% irrelevant.

What defines 'what you are' is something altogether different, something that is far more weighty and yet is completely intangible – your religion.

Ass Monkey and I were both christened Catholic Irish children by our respective parents and went to Catholic schools, but we've both somewhat, erm, 'grown out of it' along the way. Nothing terrible happened to either of us; we didn't get food poisoning from a dodgy 'body of Christ' at mass, or trip going up the aisle at our communions in front of our classmates. No one chastised me for forgetting the words to the 'Hail Mary' as Gaeilge and no one forced Ass Monkey into being an altar boy. There's no weird backstory.

But between abuse scandals and the gross display of wealth while so many people in the world have suffered and starved to death, the fact that I love my gay and lesbian friends and family that the Church 'disregards', on top of the fact that I'm a woman with a big gob who the Church treats as subservient – we, errrr, just decided in the end that it was all a bit shit really and gave it up.

Our decision on the matter didn't cause us any moral issues until Jacob came along. Ass Monkey and I quite happily spent our Sunday mornings suffering from hangovers and catching up on The X Factor (a terrible combination, by the way, resulting in serious sobbing sessions from me and staring sessions *at* me, from him), rather than going to mass. And we were fine with it.

We had only ourselves to think about and were quite happy not to have any of the existential answers that organised religion had gladly provided for us as children. Instead, we discussed science and the universe late into the night and came to other conclusions by ourselves.

Whenever we therefore mentioned to other parents that we weren't planning on having Jacob christened, surprisingly, the response was always the same, no matter who we spoke to,

'But won't you have trouble getting him into schools?'

What schools? The kind of schools that won't want our gorgeous child because he didn't go through a bullshit ceremony that announces to all his family how much 'original sin' he was born with?! Er, non merci! We shan't be bothering with that, no bleedin' way, we said.

So we opted for a non-denominational ceremony at the Unitarian Church at St. Stephen's Green in Dublin. It's called a 'Naming Ceremony', where you welcome your child to the world, bless his eyes, ears, hands and heart, invite members of the family to say a few words if they wish. He is then presented with a flower to symbolise the beauty of life and a little tiny globe of the world to represent all that the little babs will inherit.

It's awesome - all about the little person and those who love them, and not anything else. So as not to piss off our parents, who are still more or less practising Catholics (and, to be honest, to confuse them slightly), we called it 'Jacob's Baptism'. We reckoned if we didn't mention it, no one would be any the wiser that it wasn't a 'real christening'.

'Invite everyone!' Ass Monkey declared.

We did. And that was our first mistake.

Ass Monkey has a big family. Like nine sisters – NINE – and two brothers (I know, I should have checked first before taking him on) - so obviously we invited all of them, and all of my family, our friends, workmates past and present, aunts, uncles, cousins, people we went to school with, burlesque babes from the shows I'd hosted over the years, The Gays, The Straights, The Tattooed Ones… I even threw in an ex-boyfriend or two for good measure.

So when the church called to say that one of their congregation had passed away and they had to change the time of our ceremony to an hour earlier, I had to notify about eighty people with about two days notice. No stress at *all*….

With my new Momma curves, I got myself a sexy 50s dress and popped off to the hairdressers that morning for a 'curly blow-dry'. Granted, it was a Saturday morning and they were busy, but I had booked in, so when I described the look I was going for – you know, a few curls that you might just pin up back off my forehead in a retro style – I couldn't help but question internally if my hairdresser's over-exaggerated audible sighs were really warranted.

Before I continue, I need to plant something in your (well groomed) head. When I was in my late teens, circa 1992, I hung out with a couple of young ones from Finglas and picked up their style as my own. This particular fashion trend was commonly known as 'The Tracker Knacker' – shiny, colourful tracksuits, dodgy perms, and a humongous fringe held high in the sky with a million tons of hairspray.

Oh and gold sovereign rings, Johnny Blues and a shit attitude. My parents didn't let that phase go on too long, let me tell you. They actually sat me down and offered me a large sum of cash to return to my angsty Tori Amos, wailing-alone-in-my-room-for-hours phase, because it was 100% less offensive.

Anyway, that was the early nineties, and I was only a youngster, but this was now 2012, where fashion and beauty had made huge scientific and developmental leaps. Be that as it may, a shit hairdresser is still a shit hairdresser, and on the morning of my son's naming ceremony, this particular shit hairdresser sent me off out of the salon looking like it was *still* 1992. No joke.

Don't fret, I'm not completely bonkers – I did not go to the ceremony looking like an extra from the market in *Eastenders*, I did a little number on it myself to make it presentable. Was it difficult to just tease out the curls and pop two hair clips in to hold it back from my face? Was it fuck.

And the crazy bitch had actually tried to charge me extra for the 'up style' as I left the salon. I activated my asshole shield and refused access to said attempt. Over my dead image, said I.

On the way to the church in the taxi, I had another disaster. In the unforgiving glare of daylight, I glanced down at my outfit and discovered to my horror that my dress wasn't pink and black at all as thought – it was pink and navy.

So my black shoes just looked fucking stupid with it. Ass Monkey and Jacob made for the church while I ran to Zara, grabbed a new pair of shoes and hot-footed it back to them just in time for the ceremony.

May I take this opportunity to say that both Ass Monkey and Jacob looked amazing and didn't have one fashion malfunction between them. Just mammy. Always just mammy.

The ceremony was beautiful as hoped, with great speeches from Ass Monkey, godfather Noel and my dad. Not normally one to shy away from speaking in public, you'll be amaaaazed to hear that I voted myself out of this one and let Ass Monkey have his moment. He rocked it ;o)

By the time we'd walked the five hundred metres from church to restaurant for the grub, my feet were bleeding into my new shoes. Thankfully, a chemist beside the restaurant came to the rescue and my once fabulous outfit now looked like this from the top down: a half-arsed retro up-do followed by a shiny face, then a shit-hot dress on a sweaty body (it was June and I'd done an unnecessary amount of running around), into ridiculously high shoes with corners of flesh-coloured plasters peeking out of either side. Classy.

Despite being unable to get around for full-on chats with everyone who was there, the whole thing went pretty well overall. We had a face painter to keep the kids happy and the staff kept everyone's food and drink flowing. We kept Jacob entertained and made sure everyone was being looked after, and tried to be good hosts by chatting to friends and family and thanking them for coming and for bringing gorgeous presents, we posed for photos with Jacob and his cake, took group photos with family who had travelled from abroad, smiling, smiling, keeping a watchful eye on that uncle who was still insisting on smoking cigars right by where the kids were getting their faces painted, smiling…

…And then we started smoking again.

We had both been off the cigarettes since we found out that I was pregnant - Jan 2011 to then, June 2012. A year-and-a-half.

Ass Monkey was kind enough to quit with me – he of course found it incredibly easy, I found nicotine to be my one and only pregnancy craving (I even dreamt about smoking sometimes, and then would wake up feeling guilty that I had actually *been* smoking and I was a terrible mother-in-the-making).

But somewhere between dealing with the church, the ridiculous number of guests, the food, the balloons, the face painting and the crap hairdressers...it all just became too much.

I was the first to break, sweaty hand outstretched to one of my brothers, pleading with him to hand his packet of cigs over. I just had to get out of there. And on the day of my son's Naming Ceremony, I took my 'ladylike' self out to street at the front of the restaurant and sucked viciously on a fag; with my shiny forehead, my ridiculous hair and my wretched, bloody feet.

Moments later, Ass Monkey shuffled out beside me and squeezed my hand, a Silk Cut burning away in the other.

'Never again babe?'

'Never, ever, ever again,' I agreed and attempted to gracefully stub out my cigarette butt àla Olivia Newton-John in *Grease*, only to have it get stuck in a corner of a wayward foot plaster and burn a hole right there on my stupid sweaty ankle.

Chapter Twelve
BOUNCING BIRTHDAY BONANZA

'Invite everyone!' Ass Monkey declared, as Jacob's first birthday party drew near.

I exhaled ciggie smoke out of the conservatory door (once you have one...), trying to figure out how to tell my baby daddy that he'd completely lost his mind.

We'd finally moved out of our apartment when Jacob was six months old and into a big old house closer to the city. It made sense for us at the time because the bulk of our customers were restaurants and bars in town, and Ass Monkey could be spared a three-hour return trip to and from home every day.

It also meant he was spared distressed calls from New Mother Me at 6 p.m. every evening, one-way conversations which mostly went along the lines of this, 'Where the fuck are you? Jacob has started teething, Pearl has shit all over the floor, I haven't had a second to look in a mirror all day never mind take a shower. I wanted to get to the shops but I didn't get to the shops so I'm now having rice and tinned peas for dinner again. Oh and I think I have shit in my hair, I can't look. Please. Come. Home.'

Usually, 6 p.m. was only the beginning of some of Ass Monkey's calls out on the road, when he was operating as the sole engineer in the company and restaurants and bars needed their kitchen equipment to run perfectly for dinner service.

Some days, he didn't get home until 10 or 11 p.m. at night. At which point not only had he missed Jacob all day, but this lunatic of a woman that he had once regarded as his fun girlfriend, was wild-eyed, wild-haired, exhausted and incapable of carrying out a normal conversation.

We were both exhausted, so we had to make a change for the better and that change came in the form of renting a bigger space in the city.

Our new neighbours were just on the right side of bonkers. On one side was a young family with two boys who consistently kicked their footballs over the fence by accident and always wanted to see 'Jake' to give him a wave. Their parents only seemed mildly interested in our existence and rarely spoke to us, aside from the odd awkward moment when all four of us might find ourselves in our respective back gardens at the same time (The walls weren't high enough on that side to even remotely pretend that we couldn't see each other).

On the other side was a retired couple, who were delighted to have our chatty heads living next door to them, because they were chatty heads themselves. They had kept a good neighbourly eye out for the woman who owned the house we were renting, until she had gotten too ill and needed to go to a nearby nursing home for around-the-clock care.

'She never had any children,' our neighbour Olga informed us at our front gate one afternoon, shaking her head. 'But she was a school teacher and loved kids, loved her nieces and nephews. All her brothers and sisters died from polio, you know.'

'In the house?!' I gulped, horrified.

'They got sick there, yes and all went up to the children's hospital in the Phoenix Park to die....'

Jesus wept! We had only just moved in and now wondered if we were living in an Irish version of *American Horror Story: Haunted House* (we had just started watching the series and were constantly SHITTING ourselves). I knew that polio existed as a disease a long time ago, and I knew I wasn't overly suspicious but holy shitballs, we decided that the gaf couldn't have great 'Juju' or whatever.

So we immediately went indoors to light candles and incense and check under the stairs for any creepy kid-like ghosts who were searching for their missing dollies so they could finally 'go into the light'. *Shudder*. It was mostly all clear, aside from the odd inexplicable item crashing onto the floor from the cupboards or photo frames falling off the walls. I had to faux-joyfully conclude that it was due less to infantile poltergeists living with us and just shit stacking & DIY work from us.

A few weeks into our moving into the house, I had a couple of friends, Amy and Paul, over for lunch and to see Jacob. It was a gorgeous sunny day so we set up deck chairs out the back garden and ate our food there.

The three of us were chatting away and stuffing our faces, our favourite thing in the world to do. Amy and Paul were taking giddy selfies with Jacob and uploading them online immediately for all their friends and connections to see (they're younger and have infinitely more energy than I do. I tend to take the odd pic, and store them in higgledy-piggledy fashion on my phone until it either explodes from over-exertion on the storage front, or someone steals it and I lose everything).

I was happily listening to their news and gossip and shoving fistfuls of Meanies into my gob when there was a sudden halt to the hyperactive conversation.

I came up for air and saw their mildly amused faces staring over and beyond my head to the retired couple's house behind me. I followed Amy and Paul's gaze to the ridiculously tall garden wall, to discover that Fintan, Olga's rather portly and now out-of-breath, husband had shimmied up atop it. There he was, red-faced and beaming, perilously perched, and waving at us.

'I'm locked in,' he announced merrily, seemingly not at all upset by this fact.

'Oh shite,' says I. 'Would you like me to call someone for you? Or do you want my mobile phone to call someone?'

He shook his head no and stopped smiling. I looked closer: he was not only red-faced but sweating a lot and all of a sudden, he didn't seem all that well to me. He was a bit incoherent, so I thought he had maybe just had a stroke. I got myself on high alert, what was that acronym again to read the signs? K.I.S.S.? No, no, that was Keep It Simple, Stupid. (Or had I made that up?)

'She's gone off with the young lad to bring him to the shop or something, and left with the keys,' he informed us.

I thought we'd already covered that.

'Got it,' I told him. 'What can I do to help you, Fintan?'

He wobbled a little bit from atop his perch on the wall. I could hear an audible gasp from Amy and Paul – simultaneously and in beautiful harmony; they are in panto together every year – before he steadied himself again.

Oh! Oh! F.A.S.T. That was it – from the telly campaign. So the 'F' stands for 'Face - has it fallen down one side?

I squinted through the sunlight and tried to get a good look at Fintan's face. Hard to tell – it was definitely sweaty, I'd give him that. And his original greeting smile had not only fallen but completely disappeared now; did that count?

My thumb was twitching nervously over my mobile phone. I know I didn't know these people very well, and we'd just moved in, but clearly I was now responsible for this man's wellbeing, wasn't I? I was going to have to call an ambulance, the fire brigade to get through the front door, bundle everyone into the car and find his wife, wasn't I?

A. What the hell was the A for? Allergies? Arrest, as in Cardiac Arrest? No, surely that would be a 'C' then and not an 'A'. Oh fuck it, I couldn't remember. 'S'? Speech! Was his speech slurred? Only one way to find out.

'Fintan,' I repeated, more sternly this time, in the manner of Nurse Jackie from hit tv show, er, *Nurse Jackie*. 'What can I do to help you?'

As quick as a flash, he had his answer.

'I was hoping you might have a bottle of wine,' says he.

Slurred speech: check. But now at least I had a non-medical reason why. Of course I had a bottle of wine! It was a sunny Wednesday afternoon, what could be nicer for a retired man who is locked into his house than to have a crisp bottle of white wine to enjoy out his back garden?

I dragged a chair to the wall on our side and reached up to hand one to the poor, locked-in-and-thirsty man and off he shimmied back down to his own garden with his loot.

'Bad move, Sharyn,' Amy chastised me, shaking her head after he left.

My good deed for the day, perhaps actually that entire month, was already getting a beating. And this is why I'm not nice to anyone, I thought.

'What do you mean?' I vaguely tried to stand my ground, but Amy is not one to be messed with when making a point. We all became acutely aware of that when we tried to dissuade her from eating an entire bucket of Ass Monkey's infamous chicken wings. She will not be told.

'That is like giving a cat a saucer of milk. You know, a cat? Miaow? A CAT, Sharyn? A stray cat that, everyone knows, you shouldn't feed. I'm telling you – he'll be back.'

I looked at Paul – surely the gay one in our lunchy union would approve of my enabling some afternoon hooch drinking? Alas, he looked somber too.

'Sharyn,' he tutted. 'He's not locked out of his house, he's locked INTO his house. Now think about it – how do you get locked into your house?'
'Emmmmm…' I was confused.

Usually Amy and Paul were the mad buzzers and I was 'The Mammy' and I gave them advice about the world. What. Was. Happening? I slowly reached for my lunch roll to shove back in my gob where it belonged. Quick as a flash, Paul slapped it from my hand to the blanket below.

'Use your head Sharyn!' he demanded. 'It's not rocket science. In fact, it's not even Junior School science!'

I did what I did in most situations I didn't want to be in: hoped that I could use Jacob as an excuse to get out of it. I looked at him in his high chair – did he need something? Was his nappy wet? Could he at least cry like he normally did? Alas, nothing; he was happily munching on some crackers and if I'm not mistaken, was enjoying our little exchange.

Paul was not letting me away without answering this one. He wanted answers and he wanted them now. God, these two panto queens are really asserting their authority today, I thought.

'You get locked INTO your house…' I started and stuttered, 'If someone…locks you in?'

Paul and Amy, my two wise seers, looked at me with pity.

 'Exactly,' they chimed in chorus, shaking their heads sadly at this slow, clueless woman. I'm 98% sure Paul took the high note that time.

Twenty minutes later, Fintan had shimmied up the wall again, wondering if perhaps I might have a bottle of red. I couldn't even look Amy in the eye, knowing that she'd have her smug 'I know an Alco cat when I see one' head on her.

'Sorry Fintan, we don't have any red in the house. We don't really drink (Huge lie. We had a toddler, of course we drank. We had to get through it somehow), so that's that I'm afraid.'

I looked him right in the eye, hoping he'd believe me and that we wouldn't get into any argy-bargy. He stared back, wobbling again, this time presumably because he'd just necked a bottle of wine to himself in twenty minutes and was once again perched atop a very high wall that not even I would have a go at scaling.

'No problem,' he finally mumbled, and got ready to make his descent. He gave us all a big, happy wave before looking somewhere in the vicinity that I was standing in and adding, 'You're a lovely person, Siobhán.'

7UP shot out of Paul's nose as he snorted, and I'm pretty sure Amy started to choke on a carrot stick. They've been calling me Siobhán ever since.

After a week or two of mild mortification and slight avoidance on our neighbour's part, we all got over it, and after that, Fintan and Olga became our firm friends. I have to admire a man who will go to great personal trouble both physically and emotionally, to get something that he wants.

And I seriously had to admire the woman who locked him INTO the house in the first place.

The back garden in this new house of ours was humongous - at least eight-foot long - and we took great pleasure in tidying it, and planting a little veggie patch, and generally looking after it. So when Jacob's first birthday was coming up in September, Ass Monkey would hear no arguments against hiring the biggest bouncy castle that he could find.

'But we don't have to invite everyone, do we? Do you remember the baptism? The one where we started smoking again? You were there. It was awful,' I reminded him.

'Ah yes, ok, maybe not everyone, just the families then,' he agreed, before quickly adding, 'and one or two friends,' before darting off into another room.

I've already mentioned Ass Monkey's enormous family, right? With eleven siblings, some of whom have partners, and some of those couples have kids – you're already looking at the general population of a small village in Roscommon with his side alone.

My side are smaller by about a quarter, but then I have all these pals who I love and I like them to come everywhere with me, so they got invited too of course.

So as not to seem like royal asswipes who are lording a humongous bouncy castle over everyone in the area, we had to invite the neighbours' kids to be nice and then some of their friends…and then some friends who were invited had to bring their partners, and kids, and even some kids that weren't theirs but who they happened to be babysitting that weekend…and all of a sudden, we were looking at about fifty people without even trying.

Never one to be outdone in the food department, Ass Monkey would not commit to a cold buffet and sandwiches in the garden, but insisted on bringing an actual catering fryer from work into our kitchen and lashing out chicken nuggets and chips. He'd also put together one of his 'ham specials' and had to bring a commercial slicer into the kitchen, to slice the ham 'professionally'. I wish I were joking.

With the kitchen pretty much disabled with over-sized commercial kitchen equipment, rendering it impossible to function in any other normal capacity, much less move around in, it was rather difficult to even organise a bowl of cereal for oneself. I'm sure you get the picture. Sharyn's nice homely baker's-style kitchen out, Ass Monkey's better-than-a-restaurant commercial kitchen in.

To add insult to How-Am-I-Supposed-To-Ice-The-Cake injury, Ass Monkey then got called off to work the morning of the ridiculous party that we swore we wouldn't have and only got back with half an hour to spare before the guests arrived.

So by 10 a.m. that morning, in between fielding calls, getting myself and Jacob ready, cleaning the house and setting it up for the party, it was already the most stressful day ever.

We got through it, but barely, with only a few minor hiccups along the way, which were as follows:

1.   One of Ass Monkey's nephews caught me smoking behind the bouncy castle, which resulted in various lies akin to being a teenager and getting caught smoking by your parent. 'I'm just holding it for Uncle Stephen' etc.

2.   One guest fell asleep in the sitting room and started snoring like a steam train, mid-actual conversation with one of my brothers, and we had to evacuate everyone to another room so that they could actually hear themselves speak. If ever there was a more direct way to say 'Your party blows', I'd like to hear it.

3.   The kid from next door made Jacob cry by banging on his head too roughly after we sang happy birthday to him. And then I made him cry when I told him off a little too sternly. And then his mother had to call in and, erm, maybe we'll skip this bit.
4. I told one of Ass Monkey's sisters that I'd bring her a glass of water in a minute…and she's still waiting to this day (sorry Sharon x)

I can't say I recommend big birthday parties for little baby kids AT ALL. I honestly don't know why we bothered – we were stressed to the hilt and Jacob will never remember it.

When he turned two the following year? We had eight adults and three kids at the house for a slice of cake and a sup of tea and even that was too much ;o)

Chapter Thirteen
EDUCATING MONICA

I've always been a bit of a 'Monica', you know, from *Friends* - a clean freak. I'm not even entirely sure where I got it from, to be honest. Growing up, we didn't live in a very unclean home or an exceptionally clean home for that matter. It was just normal. My mam had four kids, unfortunately three of them happened to be boys, so there was a constant mucky and messy chaos all around us.

The house was stacked to the brim with football boots, football jerseys, socks, bits of broken go-carts shoved around by the back door that the boys were 'working on'. A pool table that Santa brought one Christmas that we absolutely had no room for, took up so much space in our playroom that the pool cues whacked off the walls every time you tried to take a shot.

On every conceivable inch of floor in the hallways were buckets, spades, shovels, towels caked in sand from spending all day at the nearby beaches of North County Dublin during the summer, tennis rackets and hurling sticks.

In the kitchen, it was a Soda Stream, ice pops made with water and Kia Ora dripping out of plastic containers in the freezer. In the sitting room, you could find Monopoly, Kerrr-Plunk!, Mouse Trap, all of which were missing essential pieces required for playing each game.

Our childhoods were a veritable feast of all things active and exciting and fun (even minus any modern technology that seems to both enhance and hinder kids so much these days). The memories seem happily cluttered – full of adventure and games and activities – so where amongst all that did I find the time to turn into a mini OCD clean-a-holic?

Surely I was too busy racing my brothers around the block on our bikes to prove that girls were infinitely superior to boys, to find the time to indulge in some light household duties?

Or wasn't I was so immersed in catching crabs in rock pools on the beach that I couldn't be distracted by the haphazard manner in which my mother folded the towels in the hot press?

Not so! Apparently I was pre-programmed to give a shit about the housework. Perhaps I was reincarnated to this life from being a 1950s housewife, who eventually got so fucked off vacuuming, darning socks and washing the windows in a perfectly turned out twin set and pearls, that she eventually drowned herself face-first in a homemade crème brulee and has now come back because she/I can't rest peacefully knowing what a mess I made of the kitchen floor when I eventually croaked it?

As a child, I seemed to equate cleaning the house with doing something nice to please my mother and would round up the boys when I was eleven or twelve to make the house look nice for her when she came home back from the shops.

I'm sure my time would have been better spent catching bumble bees in jam jars. If I'd been born a rich kid, I probably would have just paid for my mam to have a cleaner. One who washed and ironed the entire Under-10s GAA kit and didn't at all comment while the eldest daughter was distracted, crying at the coming out episode of *Ellen* because she was convinced that she was a lesbian too (We were both kind of awkward teenagers and a bit on the funny side. One *had* to wonder).

Besides the clean freak in me, I think I also had a touch of the *Extreme Makeover – House Edition*, in that I liked to look at a space and see if I could re-arrange it to make it prettier.

I once lived in a basement apartment in Toronto with my friend Peter, who came home from the pub late one night, fairly pickled, walked into our kitchen, looked around, and left again. He figured he was in the wrong apartment and stood on the street outside for a good twenty minutes while building up the courage to let himself back in to have another look.

I had spent a good six hours cleaning, reorganising and redecorating that day, so the place looked completely different and, in my estimation, much more liveable-inable.

But when I think back on it now I could have been out seeing the world, meeting people, visiting tourist hot spots. But no, I instead pulled another crazy 'Monica'.

The apartment that Ass Monkey and I lived in when we had Jacob first was an easy clean – wooden floors, a modern bathroom and a field behind the wall of the back garden that you could fling the dog shit over and into. The house we moved to in Dublin city, on the other hand, was not.

We wanted to rent it really badly because we had this misguided idea that Jacob was totally going to need the humongous back garden that went with it (he was six months old and could barely crawl at this point; idiots).

But also, I thought, What an amazing challenge!. We could spend loads of time (and some of our money) on making this rented house look really decent and wasn't that really exciting and fun? (Perhaps I was suffering from some sort of postpartum mental breakdown after all, now that I think of it).

It WASN'T fun. Let me tell you something for nothing, you something-for-nothing-seekers, HOUSEWORK IS A POX. My obsession with it is *thee* most boring thing about myself. I wasted so much time cleaning this too-old and too-dirty rented house we had chosen, that I should have spent going on play dates, walking in the park to see the ducks, writing, having conversations with other actual human beings, sleeping when Jacob was sleeping, or lying down on the couch watching Cagney and Lacey re-runs. Anything but.

I think now that I was weirdly obsessed with cleaning. I so desperately didn't want my baby to crawl around on a dirty carpet that I found myself one morning, in my dressing gown, on hands and knees, scrubbing stains out of the carpet with a basin of water and a nail brush. It was 6 a.m.

'That's it!' I announced, to no one in particular, because everyone else who was reasonable was in bed. 'We'll have to get a cleaner.'

A handwritten note had come through the door a few days earlier, offering cleaning services, which is what had put the idea in my head. So I called later that day, and got Katarina, Russian and totally friendly on the other end of the line. We arranged for her to come later in the week.

When Katarina arrived, I couldn't help myself but blink in delight and surprise at her ridie Amazonian-ness. She was tall and super-skinny, with a long mane of fiery red hair, that reminded me of the kind of loose perm and top-heavy layered cut that I had gotten for my confirmation when I was twelve and looked like Mufasa from *The Lion King*.

Katarina didn't wear a scrap of make-up except for liquid eyeliner in a metallic grey that started in the inside corner of her eye and ended somewhere around her ear lobe. She was amazing to look at and had a wonderful gentle nature, one that didn't match her look at all. If I'm honest, I would have felt much more like the world was in order if she'd been a professional hit woman.

I told Katarina that I just really needed help to straighten this crazy house out and couldn't do it alone, so she scoured my cupboards for cleaning products (all present), donned the Marigolds and set off to work.

On those days that she was in the house, I wheeled Jacob out to the front or back garden and tried to tame the crazy trees, bushes and hedges.

They were so wild that it took nearly the entire year we stayed there to sort them out. Why we bothered, I'd like to say 'no one knows', but it was undoubtedly because I was going batshit crazy over the state of them and didn't want to be 'mortified' if some friends or family were to come by. Like anyone else ever noticed.

(Actually, this isn't true. This is what I say to people who are worried about other people judging them on the cleanliness of their houses and I want them to feel better.

But people do notice. Some just understand more than others when your house is upside down and would never dream of making you feel bad about it, some people are a bit tactless and might politely enquire if the liquid seeping from under the refrigerator door is in fact blood of some sort. Fair enough.

And some people, the ones who criticise the artwork on your wall as being 'lazy', or comment that some carpet stains are nearly impossible to remove and 'oh. my. GOD. I have the number of a great window washer that I must give you' – are just assholes.

Then there are the ones who love you no matter what: my mother and I have a running joke about inspecting the cleanliness of each other's toilets because she stayed with me in my apartment once, used the jacks, came back out and announced with a smirk, 'I just gave that a little scrub for you.' The wagon ;o))

My relationship with Katarina was going great until two things happened:

1. She started telling me all of her problems, and
2. She stopped wearing a bra to our house.

Now. I am and have always been one of those people who enjoys talking to people about their bad day. I take the time to enquire about their sleepy-looking face, I drag the real story out of why someone has elbow psoriasis and why they can't stand goldfish.

It invariably ends up with that person and I crying together, promising to be friends forever and recommending self-help books to each other. I am also the person that random strangers tell their life stories to, whether I've gone to the trouble of asking or not.

I'll get sitting beside someone I've never met before at a hens dinner, for example, who will blurt out that they've never forgiven their stepdad for leaving them out of their will, and I end up mopping up their mascara-streaked faces in the toilets for two hours. And I kinda like it that way, always have. It's my buzz.

However, I was very narked when we moved to this new house. My kid wouldn't sleep, I was running our company office from the front living room and had to literally run there every time Jacob went for a half-hour snooze, so that I could get as much done as possible in order that the business wouldn't fall down around us. I wasn't exactly in the market for 'White Oprah-esquing' at the time, but still – STILL it came.

'I told my mother I am very worried that you are not happy with me,' Katarina announced one morning as she bleached the bejaysus out of the kitchen (I loved that she did that, window and all, but you'd have needed a gas mask to stay alive and I certainly didn't want Jacob near the chemical high. He was happily snoozing in his buggy in the sunny back garden though).
  'Erm, why is that?' I tentatively enquired, reaching for the watering cans.

In my mind, so long as she kept re-arranging my kitchen window ledge in that military-precision way that she did, she could stay forever. But I wasn't opposed to waving the gardening gloves and watering cans and cheerily yelling, 'Hi ho, hi ho, it's off to the garden I go,' when I'd had enough.
'I think I am not quick enough for you. My mother tells me 'Then go faster!'

Katarina laughed and I laughed. And then I was vaguely aware that she had popped her cloth down into the bleach bucket and was casually leaning back against the kitchen counter top to have this chat with me and I thought *Really? Are you going to stop working to tell me you're worried that I'm worried that you're not working hard enough?*

'You're doing a great job,' I reassured her, trying to move off to get back out to the garden.

'Oh good,' Katarina nods as she places a Marigold-free hand on my arm. 'Because, you know, I have to put my kid through to tennis camp. She will be professional. I do this myself, there is no one else to make money. There is no man.'

For effect, she shook her Mufasa-inspired-head sadly from side to side.

There it was: GUILT TRIP. Strike One.

The following week, Katarina showed up to the house and it was beyond obvious that she had elected not to wear a bra that day. Not obvious in a 'and she also forgot to wear a TOP' kind of a way, OR that her boobs were particularly massive.

No, she had ickle boobs like mine, so I know that you can totally get away with not wearing a bra, but you must also take the time to layer up in case your nip-nips decide to make their presence known for any reason.

But Katarina – Amazonian, flamed-haired, wonderful Katarina, appeared to be wearing what can only be described as a Penneys vest –for a six-year-old. It was one of those dusty pink ones, ribbed and with a tiny pink bow at the neck. It was so small on her frame that she wore it like a belly top – like a really, REALLY almost see-through thin belly top.

Ass Monkey was at home doing a bit of work in the office that morning and couldn't quite figure out where to look when she landed in on top of him to ask, 'Hoover here?'

'No, no thanks, not necessary!' he trilled, staring straight at the floor in case he'd be rendered blind from staring directly at her big Russian, recently released nipples.

We agreed later on that evening that it was a fluke, an accident - that she had merely forgotten her bra that day, sure it could happen to anyone and we wouldn't worry too much about it. But it was the same story the next time she arrived and the next time. NO BRA.

I kept thinking, we're in the middle of a recession, we have a new baby – I actually need my boyfriend to go OUT to work and you're not helping, Thunder Tits.

Eventually, I had to do the only decent, upstanding thing I knew to get out of our weird, uncomfortable situation (I mean, only for us; Katarina was clearly very comfortable in her bra-free state), I had to lie. I told her we were going on holiday for two weeks and that I'd text her when we got back. And then…eeek…I didn't text her.

I'm sorry Katarina. I hope you, your mother, your kid and your boobies are all well. And I thank you for teaching me the most valuable lesson I could have learned that year: that the housework REALLY isn't worth getting your bra in a twist over.

Chapter Fourteen
CRECHE BANG WALLOP

By the time Jacob had turned one, I was pretty sick of him. Hahaha, only joking, honestly! (* can you hear the hysterical laughter of a lying woman?!*) We had spent a full year together, hanging out, while I tried to simultaneously keep my 'Sharyn Life' on track – this is the one that has nothing to do with Ass Monkey or Jacob or running the family business.

It's the writing, the performing, the going on courses and to auditions – when either Ass Monkey would skid up to the curb in his van and take Jacob for an hour, or friends or family would step in. Or I'd have to pay someone to be the surrogate Mammy Me until I got back from vying for a baby puke-and-shit-free experience.

It was a bit of a complicated time, in hindsight, and as a baby, Jacob was dragged around the town and country a lot for the sake of my whimsical fantasies of *'Even though I'm a Mother Now, It's Cool – Nothing Has To Change. Right?'*

Ass Monkey and I started looking at local crèches for consistent child-minding options when Jacob was about eleven months old. I asked around and friends of ours recommended the one that their daughter was in (well, one would hope so, wouldn't one?) so we visited there.

And it was lovely: clean, colourful, the staff was all smiley and polite, the children seemed to have plenty of freedom to run around and there was a cool outdoor garden.

But there was another crèche that was closer to our house. So close, that I could wheel him down there in the morning and bring Pearl with me. I could literally have the morning dog walk down in conjunction with the kid drop off and then I could get home to start my day all before 9 a.m.! We made an appointment to see them too, as soon as possible.

On our appointed day, we rocked up with Jacob and were greeted by a crossed-eyed and full-of-snot kid with his face pressed right up against the glass window in a room at the front. Yes. Like he was a patient there. Ass Monkey and I shared a nervous glance, 'Weird, right?'

Once inside, the staff seemed startled to see us and we were told that the manageress must have forgotten about our appointment, but sure no problem, that we could come in anyway for a look around.

I took a quick peek in the room where the snotty kid had been staring at us, One Flew Over The Cuckoo's Nest-style, out of the window. There were a few other kids besides our 'Greeter' roaming around and erm, no adults to speak of in there to look after them and em, just a locked stair gate keeping all the little kiddies inside.

Amazed, we followed our guide past a staff room on the way upstairs, where two or three women stared grumpily out at us from under their misery at a little staff table. I know that this cannot be true, but in my memory, I somehow recall them as scowling there and smoking, perhaps contemplating extinguishing their butts on the arm of some wayward kid. The whole thing had a bit of a Dickensian workhouse feel to it.

We – at this point, reluctantly and with a protective hand over Jacob's eyes lest our baby thought we would actually contemplate leaving him there - made a move to the first floor, where one girl with a *prison tattoo* on her neck was solely responsible for two roomfuls of kids 'because de rest o' de gurls are on der breaks.'

We fooking legged it. I called Crèche Number One back, and begged them for a part-time place for Jacob. The manageress advised that there wasn't just one at that time. Gutted, I pondered my predicament for a day or two, trying to come up with another solution.

It wasn't a matter of life or death if Jacob didn't get into a crèche straight away, I didn't exactly have a full-time job to 'go to' or anything since I mostly worked from home - but it sure would make life a teeny bit easier. Aside from that, to give us our dues as parents, we wanted him to interact with other kids as opposed to spending all his time with his ma and his dog.

As is often the case, the answer came to me in the middle the night, as I suffered yet another punch straight to the nipple from our darrrrling sleeping babe in the bed between us.

I stretched an arm over Jacob and poked Ass Monkey in his ribs.

'Ow! What's that for?'
'You'll have to take this one for the team, I'm afraid.'
'What one? What team?' he mumbled from underneath his pillow. He always sleeps with a pillow on his head. Something to do with my snoring, he says. I have ASTHMA, I'll have you know.

I pulled the pillow from his face, because I'm lovely like that.

'Tomorrow. You have to get dressed up, like, in your cleanest work wear, but you'll have to actually wash, and put hair gel in, not just my body lotion like you usually do and maybe spray a bit of Issey Miyake on yourself. You have to hang a few tools – spanners and the likes – from your tool belt, maybe throw a clean pencil behind your ear for effect. And you'll have to go down to that crèche we like.'

Neither Ass Monkey nor any other living human being can sleep through my high-pitched rants when I get going, so he rolled over and stared at me through big long sleepy eyelashes.

'And do what?' he asked. 'They said there was no place for Jacob, so there's obviously no place.'

'Don't be ridiculous. There's always a place. They just need to want to give it to us. So tomorrow, you will go down there, you'll knock on the door, you'll give them your best James Dean-slash-Colin Farrell-slash-stroke victim side-smile that you can muster up and you will flirt with those women until they change their minds.'

'But I – '

'No arguments,' I cut him off, palm up in the air. 'There is absolutely no value in my going out with a ride like you if I can't pimp you out from time to time.'

Ass Monkey, AKA The Ride, valiantly took one for the team the next day and dropped into the crèche to investigate 'when a place might come up in the future?'

I got a phone call that afternoon from the manageress who said she'd look into it and come back to us as soon as possible. Result! The power of that man's hair and crinkly-eyed smile knows no bounds.

But I still hadn't heard from them after another few weeks, and so I took matters a little bit further, a little bit lower you might say, and sent this email in:

Dear Gill,
I hope you are having a nice day.
Pretty please, can you see if there is some space in your crèche for me in September, because I really, really like it

and want to make friends with the other cute little people there.
Lots of love,
Jacob xxx

Manipulative much, Sharyn? Well, who could resist an email from an actual baby? We finally got Jacob into the crèche two days a week and I couldn't have been happier.

At this point, we were just over a year and a half into running the engineering firm together, and so Ass Monkey was still out ten to twelve hours a day on the road, and I was doing the accounts from home.

To be honest, I was really only skimming the surface of the accounts because I never had a full run at it, so this was our chance to get things a little more organised.

The first week or so were really hard leaving Jacob behind, and I tended to drop him off late and pick him up early. But slowly and surely, he and I both grew in confidence with our new routine.

I got to know the girls really well and totally loved them from the get-go. In fact, I was so relieved to have some actual time to myself again, that I kept telling them all how much I loved them. I'm pretty sure that made them rather uncomfortable, but I couldn't hide my joy in it. Mammy had a break at last!

They really did care about Jacob, and all the other kids in the crèche were genuinely happy to see us walk in the door (and leave too, I'm sure!). I didn't hold back in any way with throwing cakes and goodies into them and telling them how amazing they were on a regular basis (as should everyone who has their kids minded. If the minder likes you, they will like your kid by extension. That is your Sharyn Not-Based-In-Any-Scientific-Fact... Fact for the day).

As an extra treat, I also sent Ass Monkey in from time to time to do the pickup or drop-off and see the girls. I have it on good advice that when the girls 'rated the dads', he was up there at the top of their list ;o)

The only downside was that Jacob, tough and all as he was, was now exposed to lots of other kiddies which of course meant lots of other kiddie germs. He hadn't been at all sick aside from teething problems up until he turned one, and all of a sudden he was getting every jaysus thing, from earaches to sore throats to fevers.

For some reason, I hadn't anticipated his ever getting sick (yes, like in his entire life) and so, as usual, was totally unprepared for what was to come.

The first time he got a fever, we were totally panicked and scared for our little guy. The three of us sat outside in the cool conservatory in the middle of the night, Jacob with just his little nappy on, as we tried to cool him down.

When that didn't entirely work, I came up with Plan B and it was the worst thing imaginable – I put him into a cool bath. What the fuck was I thinking? He screamed and screamed the whole house and neighbourhood, and some sections of the Phoenix Park, down with agony, even though I thought I was doing him a favour.

FAIL. FAIL. FAIL. I totally learned something new that day: my instincts cannot be trusted at 4 a.m.

Our ignorance in this 'being responsible for a baby' lark became even more apparent, as we engaged in yet another perceived parenting 'No-No' while he was sick: we let him sleep in our bed. This is what I now refer to as 'The Year Of The Head-butt'.

Ass Monkey and I endured several hundred unwarranted assaults to our heads, chests and faces as Jacob writhed around in our bed between us at night.

Sometimes he arched his back and threw his entire little body in our direction when he was having a little meltdown about something. We'd at least be normally awake for those if he was up and screaming and could avoid the (oh my God, REALLY hard) back of his head attacks on us.

But a lot of the time, he writhed around when he – and we – were asleep, so that we endured these surprise nosebleeds, lip bleeds and sometimes, a teeny tiny, well-placed kick to the genitals. Our baby was a guerilla.

Basically, Jacob battered us and we let him, because he obviously didn't mean it (did he?), we didn't want him to be sick alone and we love him.

That said, we did then spend the following year trying to get him the fuck back out of our bed. And guess what? Yup. we're still trying.

Chapter Fifteen
WORD TO YOUR MOM'S (HOOP)

It took me a year to lose the baby weight after Jacob was born. A full year, almost to the day. I am normally at my happiest, healthiest, skin, hair-and-nails-bestest at nine stone. Despite determining to ingest a diet of only Bran Flakes and plain Digestive biscuits when I was a teenager, I was disappointingly never anorexic as hoped and my weight stubbornly remained at nine stone from the age of about eighteen until now.

Ecstasy landed on our shores right as I was hitting my late teens, and was discovering clubbing, Ibiza and all the celebrity DJs I wished to shag. I was ripe for a mild amphetamine addiction that might have contributed to the perfect 'Stripper Body' that was so thin and *so* chic. But alas, I much preferred dancing to drugging, and my over-powering vanity refused to let me chew the face off myself on E whilst rocking my neon pink PVC skirt. I mean – why ruin a perfectly well assembled outfit with a stupid-looking face?

The only time I really ever lost weight was when I got the chicken pox at the grand ol' age of twenty-nine. That's right, not the shingles, as everyone always asks: the chicken pox.

On consultation with my mother at the time, she indicated that she was 'pretty sure' that I had them as a child and promised to cast her mind back after dinner. I'm still waiting for her feedback. That I'm her first child and only daughter and she still can't remember isn't alarming at all...is it, Liz?!

I got those chicken pox everywhere, people, and I mean in every single crevice you can possibly imagine...but most of them were in my throat and threatened to close over my windpipe. This not only delighted my entire group of friends and family because it meant that I would be unable to speak for several days (at least), but it also rendered me unable to eat anything other than a diet of Ready Brek and Petite Filous for two weeks.

And at the end of that two weeks, I was seven and a half stone, right in time for Christmas. (Nothing like a pre-Christmas pox attack to get you into that tiny black dress.

I would, however, like to add that getting to seven and a half stone – for any reason – requires way too much starvation and hardship. So unless you fancy some chicken poxs' up your fandora, don't do it, ok?)

The thing is, I really like my grub, and when I was pregnant, my taste buds burst open (partly due, no doubt, to the fact that I was no longer smoking) – and I extra loved, loved, LOVED my grub. I enjoyed eating in, eating out, planning the big Sunday roast, and could most days be found with my head stuck in the fridge, scouring it for treats. I *was* active though too, so I balanced the gluttony out; I went swimming, took pre-natal yoga classes and of course, walked Pearl every day.

In those early pregnancy days, I read somewhere that an increase of about two stone by the end of the pregnancy was about right, so I set to work. I didn't take this information as a 'loose guideline' of any sort, i.e. that I could put on up to two stone and that would be ok – no, no. I took it as a *goal* to work towards and thoroughly enjoyed stuffing copious amounts of ice cream, cakes and chocolate down my gob in order to 'meet my target weight'. I was never one to turn down a challenge.

I admit I had many days where I bemoaned my odd new body shape after Jacob was born. There was no firm bump any more, that I could point to and say, 'Here! This is what that extra two stone is about!' My bump was deflated, my body was slowly easing itself back into pre-baby place, my boobs were trying to remember that they'd only ever been a modest 34B **and** I eventually had to admit that the baby had, in fact, only contributed to about half of the weight I'd put on!

I didn't try to lose it straight away – I was tired, and to me, tired = chocolate. There wasn't a 2 a.m. or 4 a.m. or, ok, a 3 p.m. feed for the baby that wasn't accompanied by some chocolate delight or other from the fridge. I mean, for God's sake, I was hungry too! I made a big song and dance about attending a hot yoga course to tone up when Jacob was a couple of months old, but if I'm honest, it was more for the sleepy lying-down bit at the end of each class than anything else. That was sooo nice.

It wasn't until we moved to the rented city centre house and I had the rolling hills of the Phoenix Park, to both simultaneously drag the dog and push the buggy up and down, that the weight began to really fall off. We went out three or four times a week for an hour long walk in total and it really did the trick.

There was also the fact that we now had a flight of stairs in this house and they, combined with my total shit memory, helped tone my ass.

I'd run up with Jacob in my arms (my personal kettle bell!) to grab nappies for his changing bag, get back downstairs to realise I'd forgotten my phone, and run back up again. That happened a lot. Hmmm…maybe I should have been a little less concerned about the progress of my ass, and more concerned about the deterioration of my *mind*. I may need to go any buy myself some fish oils.

Losing the weight and toning up was a slow and enjoyable process and quite literally, on the day that Jacob turned one, I was back to my nine stone self.

I didn't have the privilege of being able to fork out for a tummy tuck right after the baby was born like some richy-poo people, and really, I'm not sure how natural that is anyway. Friends who have had babies and are living with their baby bump for longer than they'd hope to, ask me how long it takes to get rid of all the time.

And my answer is always the same – *give yourself a break for a year afterwards.* Yes, a whole year.

I'm not saying give in to being a slob (or do, whatever makes you happy), but if you do want to lose the pregnancy weight, take your time and try not to get too upset if it doesn't drop off straight away. If you look after yourself, you *will* get to where you want it to be in time.

And remember, your body looks different after giving birth for a really good reason ;o)

For the record – I think my body is better now than it was before I got pregnant. I'm so much more proud of it because it did this super amazing thing. It gave me my son.

chapter Sixteen
DOWN AND OUT IN GRIMNAGH & GLUMLIN

Things were going pretty amazing for Ass Monkey and I at the beginning of 2013 until these two things happened:

1. Our landlord demanded an extra €100 a month in rent from us when our lease came up for renewal. A hundred euro a month extra. In a recession. In a house that we had to scrub, fix, clear out, pay through the nose for the impossible task of heating it…. Not, as one might imagine, a rent reduction for being sound, and vaguely hoping that we might stay there for another year. Lord, no.

2. Fintan, our scaling-the-wall-for-hooch-retired-pal-from-next-door, died in what can only be described as spectacular fashion. Ass Monkey and I had just sat down for dinner when Fintan's wife came banging the door down, shouting at us to 'Please come! I think he's dead.'

Ass Monkey, pale as a sheet, leapt into their front garden and into the house, and ran upstairs as I half-dragged and half-carried poor Olga in. She and I were only a quarter of the way up the stairs when Ass Monkey came back down towards us. I knew instantly from the look on his face that our friend was gone before he even said the words 'I'm so sorry' to Olga.

Fintan had had a stroke in his sleep. Ass Monkey had given up the booze for nearly a year at that point but we both necked about four hot whiskeys later on in our conservatory, candles lit, blankets on our laps, holding hands, utter sadness in our hearts.

We had one criteria for moving to a new house, and that was to go some place close to Jacob's crèche that he and I both had grown to love so much. We were down to the last two weeks before the lease in our old house was up and were getting desperate. There was nothing suitable in the area we currently lived in, and at any rate, we felt as though our luck had been pretty fucking shit there.

One of my great mates Áine, a ridie rock chick with countless tattoos and piercings, lived in nearby Drimnagh so we started looking there. The crèche was even closer to Drimnagh than it was to our other house, and Áine made promises of daytime walks and nighttime wine drinking that I couldn't possibly ignore.

We eventually found a place, much smaller than the big old other house that we didn't need, with shag-all of a garden so that I wouldn't have to worry about it. And the nicest thing– it was warm. We jumped on it immediately and moved in, marvelling at how clean the house was, how much storage it had, how everything was clearly going to be easier now….

Within days, a Russian man, claiming to be our next-door neighbour called to the front door in his Y-fronts, Crocs shoes, tatty dressing gown flailing in the wind and a cigarette butt hanging from his lips.

'Never park your van in front of my house. Ever,' he spat in Ass Monkey's face, exhaling a cloud of cigarette smoke into the front door and, as I have always imagined, spitting at his feet before departing back down the driveway (This probably didn't happen but it would be cool drama if it did).

'Pleasure to meet you too!' Ass Monkey shouted after him as he quickly slammed the door to protect Jacob and I from witnessing any of the ridiculous exchange.

We had only just moved the van out from the end of our driveway for a minute so I could get my car out. For a *minute.*

'We're fucked!' I moaned, as he recalled the encounter. 'We've moved next door to the naked Russian mafia. We've moved to GRIMnagh!'

'At least we're near the, em, Luas line?' Ass Monkey offered and promised to take me out to town at the weekend for dinner.

We'd hop in on the Luas and hop back out on the Luas, he said, and we'd wonder how we'd ever survived not living right next to the Luas up until now.

Now. For those of you who don't know, the Luas is a public transport system in Dublin that the Irish government rolled out some years back. It connects Dublin city centre with many of its external suburban areas, both south and west side.

It does not go north side, despite the promises that it might some day and despite all the people living in Finglas who like to get into town on a regular basis to go to Krystle nightclub and hang with Rosanna Davison (she is a model of the people, is she not?!. Because of broken governmental promises, those poor, glamour-seeking people still have to take the distinctly unglamorous bus in their knock-off Christian Louboutins. The shame.

The Irish government also failed to connect the south and west side Luas lines, a decision that we all determined was based on their ineptitude and lack of financial direction in managing the funds, and I joined that brigade. I did.

I said things like 'Why the jaysus would you not facilitate the people from Rialto who want to go to Dundrum Shopping Centre for the afternoon? It's not like they don't have a Penneys out there.'

But now I know why. I no longer think the government made a transportation faux pas. I think they knew exactly what they were doing and that the lack of a connection was completely intentional.

They don't want the people from Rialto, Black Horse, St. James' Hospital and beyond to get on the south side Luas. **They want to keep them away from Dundrum Shopping Centre**. It's precisely why they gave them The Square in Tallaght – it is now my theory that the government believes that the people on the Tallaght Line are not good enough for the Dundrum Line.

Until we moved to GrimNagh, I had only ever had the pleasure of travelling on the south side Luas. I had worked in an office on the south side of the city for some years and would pop out to Dundrum to catch up with mates over coffee, or to go to the cinema. Ass Monkey did a bit of work in a Chinese restaurant out there too, so we'd visit there on occasion and have dinner.

On the night that we decided to have a 'date' in town from GrimNagh, we got the west side Luas at around 8 p.m. It was March and pretty dark outside since winter had decided to extend its stay in 2013.

But it was also most normal children's bedtimes, that 8 p.m. mark. Our Jacob was being babysat by his grandparents and had most likely had a bath, a bedtime story and was just snuggling down to sleep at that point.

Other older kids, eight, nine and ten-year-olds, would have been maybe allowed stay up late to watch some TV with their parents, as it was Saturday night, but would of course be going to bed soon so that they were fresh for football/swimming/trombone lessons/visiting their cousins the next day.

Not so The Children of The Red Luas Line (Yes, this is quite like the fairy tale, *The Children of Lir*, and yes, just as grim too, if not, well, more grim).

I am pre-empting this story by telling you that I am no pussy, no sirreeeeeeee bob. Nor am I a snob. As proof, here's a confession, just for you: I once had a boyfriend in New York who was from Harlem and taught me how to use his 9 mm hand gun 'for my own protection' and I still continued to date him until my visa ran out (Angelo, where are you now? Prison?).

But on the Luas that night, there was a gang of hyperactive, angry, potentially lethal eleven-year-old girls that I was terrified of. Well, at the very least, gobsmacked at. They were running from one end of the carriage to the next, screaming in old people's faces at close range, knocking newspapers out of people's hands, and generally terrorising everyone they came into contact with.

Normally speaking, I'm lucky in that I have the extremely effective 'Don't You Dare Even Try To Fuck With Me' stare down in my arsenal and if that fails, I generally point at Ass Monkey and say, with sincerity, 'I can't believe you would act like this in front of Colin Farrell' (That normally disables their shite behaviour for long enough, as they try to figure out if Ass Monkey IS Colin Farrell, so that we can make our escape).

I didn't need either weapon that night because the little brats didn't come near us, but I did think how I'd hate to be a vulnerable elderly person in the midst of this kind of siege. And where were the fucking security dudes anyway?

Ass Monkey grabbed my hand tightly and leaned in for a pep talk:

'Efforts must be quadrupled to save every penny we can to buy our own house. Our Jacob can't end up like these kids.'

I nodded, dumbstruck, as I witnessed one of the eleven-year-olds sparking up a Johnny Blue cigarette and inhaling it like she'd already been smoking for about eight years.

'Absolutely,' I agreed. 'No child of mine will be allowed outdoors, unattended, wearing a sweater with Katie Price's face on it. Ever. Where do they even buy these things?'

Most of our neighbours in GrimNagh were pretty cool though. We were a few weeks in when I figured out how my rubbish bins were miraculously reappearing in the front garden after the bin trucks had emptied them out.

'Surely Greyhound don't offer that kind of a service now?' I wondered to myself. 'Surely not in GrimNagh?'

I eventually spotted my neighbour, on the other side from the Russians, kindly dragging my bins in. He looked like a nice older man, not too unlike Fintan, who we still missed all the time. I made a mental note not to get close to him in case he died too. We couldn't have hacked it and I don't want 'Inexplicable Killer Of Old Next-Door Neighbour Men' on my own tombstone, thank you very much.

'Menopausal Hilary' waved happily every morning from her house across the street until I paused by my car long enough to allow her to walk over and introduce herself. In case you're wondering how I know that she was menopausal, here is a broad outline of our very first interaction, ever.

'Hiya, I'm Hilary. Just think of the Clintons, and you'll never forget my name. Warm day isn't it? Of course, I have my own internal heating system going on, what with the hot flushes and all. How old is the little fella there, isn't he gorgeous? I never let my two girls out on the road here, sure you couldn't around here. It's bedlam!'

I love Menopausal Hilary. It was the best introduction to another human being that I have ever experienced.

We had another bout of sore ear/sore throat with Jacob that autumn, and were at our GP's office when we noticed a little rash on his arm. Rather than take any chances, we were advised to get it checked out straight away.

'What hospital would you like to go to?' the GP asked me.

I had no idea but guessed GlumLin (Crumlin) Children's Hospital, since it was the one closest to our new address, and she referred us on.

Don't worry, I'm not about to beat down on the hospital. The kids and parents that truly need that place deserve for me not to do that. The hospital does need work, a lot of work, and I can see why there's so much fundraising going on, on its behalf.

There are just a few little things I might mention for some improvements; they could use a full-time member of staff on the front desk so that when you arrive on a Friday evening with your kid, shitting yourself with the word 'meningitis' running riot around your head, you have someone to direct you to the right place as opposed to an empty, unmanned desk.

They could then do with giving the ladies on A&E admissions countless boxes of chocolate biscuits for being so amazing, kind and knowing where everything is. Love them.

Finally, the hospital could kindly also do with training some of their 'doctors' in how to administer a simple blood take from a toddler, so that he doesn't need to be pinned down by five people as she fucks it up, refuses to let one of the nurses to do it, instead insisting on doing it over and over again herself.

They could also use the money for their legal fees to take me to court, when I punch that doctor in the face in if I ever meet her on the street.

That is all. Our baby was fine in the end and the 'rash' was more like a long-lasting mark from something he had leaned on. This parent took considerably longer to recover than he did.

Of course, there are hilarities to living in places like GrimNagh and GlumLin, if you look for them, and happily, I seem to always attract the 'Roddy Doyle-esque' scenes of working class Dublin comedy into my real life.

For example, I went to the local shop for a few bits. There was a gang of lads hanging around outside, including one fifteen-year-old in a wheelchair.

'Howaya, gorgeous,' says he as I walked into the shops so naturally enough I give him a wink in return (No I am not that in need of compliments but who could deny the young lad's delightful personality. He also wasn't at all bad looking FYI).

On my way back out of the shop, he was waiting for me at the door and asked for my phone number.
'Oh sorry,' I chirped. 'I have a boyfriend, thanks so much for asking though!'
    I gave him another wink and a smile to be kind and let the, I was sure, crushed young man down gently.

Just as I was getting back to my car, beaming to myself at how cute he was asking for my number like that, he roared up the street after me,

'I might be in a wheelchair missus, but me willy still works!'

Things To Avoid When Dealing With New Parents

1. Posting Their News On Your Facebook Page

You got the text, and if you're known for being a big mouth, you're probably lucky that you got that text at all.

Please note, *this news does not belong to you*. Don't go all Town Crier on it and lash it up online. Leave that to the actual parents. Nobody likes a Thunder Thief.

2. Being Hungry Or Thirsty When You Visit:

If someone has just had a child, they are most likely in a current state of shock/panic/nausea/all of the above and do not need to play host to you if you call to visit. Do NOT ask for a second cup of coffee, sandwich or enquire as to what's on for dinner.

Be a dear and bring them something to eat or a takeaway coffee when you arrive. Bonus points are always given to the bringers of cake.

3. Arriving On Their Doorstep As A 'Surprise!'

This especially applies if you live abroad and if these new parents really aren't expecting you. Now that you've flown here from Taiwan or whatever, these poor people feel obliged to cater to you by feeding you and (God forbid) putting you up for a few days.

You do get that they are already doing this with a tiny new crying person, right? I'm sure in your heart you were doing something lovely and exciting, and you went to all that trouble of taking the red eye to get here right at the minute that the baby turned one week old. But listen – UNEXPECTED GUESTS ARE THE DEVIL OF NEW PARENTS' LIVES.

So unless you're,
1. Super Nanny and you've decided to move in (for free and somehow also, invisibly) for six weeks, or
2. The man who owns The Lotto and you've come to drop off an enormous cheque... **STAY. AWAY.**

4. Criticising *Anything* For At Least Six Months And/Or until Emotions Have Returned To Normal Levels.

A guest who came to visit our son when he was three weeks old, was handed a tasty beverage, took a sip and said, 'Um, this glass smells kind of garlicky?'

Perhaps that glass *was* garlicky, and this may seem like a very trivial thing for me to take personally, but I still haven't forgotten it two years on. That'd be the hormones, peeps, the raging, raging hormones.

But also, I'd still like to think that we as a species can still feign politeness, you know? Much like when the hairdresser dyes your hair candy floss green and you convincingly tell them it's amazing. Applying that skill, you could essentially take that garlicky glass and hold your nose and drink your beer that we went to the trouble of picking up at the shops for you. With our new baby in tow.

Or you could shove it slyly into the dishwasher when no one is looking and never speak of it again. Or go thirsty for half an hour. Just figure it out, ok?

5. Pausing When The New Baby's Name Is Announced.

There will be no pausing. Pausing indicates that you aren't sure about something. Like, you're not sure that these parents have made the right choice about their own baby's name and you might have a better idea yourself.

It's none of your business and you can totally abbreviate it/slag it off from the comfort of your own kitchen when you get home later like everyone else. For now – get your game face on and give the standard, polite and only acceptable answer which is, 'Oh how lovely and unusual. Tell me, is that Latin for something?

Chapter Seventeen
A LADY OF LEISURE

I once spent fifty minutes trying to buy tampons in my local shop. It was a Sunday morning, I had just brought Pearl out for a big run around the park, and stopped by the shops for the usual purchases: milk, bread, papers and, erm...tampons. Alas, there in the personal hygiene aisle stood One Of The Dads From The Crèche Jacob Attended.

We didn't know each other personally. In fact, his only communication with me up to that point, had been to nod at me suspiciously as we passed each other dropping off and collecting our kids at the centre.

But not this particular morning. Oh no, this morning, he was all of the chats. His gorgeous daughter was exploring (i.e. pulling down) the shampoo shelves, and we both kept an eye on her as he told me about the second baby who had just arrived and the visitors they were having that day.

Oh and where did I think they should move to when they bought a new house?

Uh huh, uh huh. I went from Nameless Other Parent that he had never once said a word to, to his Personal Life Advisor in sixty seconds flat. Just like that. Sound. And because it's none of my business where these strangers live and furthermore - I don't care - all I could think about the whole time he was chatting was, 'If I just pick up the box of tampons and start waving them around in front of him, gesticulating wildly like an Italian and warn him against the 'Bad End' of Drimnagh (where we had moved to at the time), then maybe he'd be mortified, stop this weird public service information request and let me get home.

I was just on the verge of putting my hand to the box of yellow regulars (I have a very average vagina, thanks for asking), when he delivered his next supersonic surprising question,

'So are you working yourself, or are you a lady of leisure?'

I...I drew a blank. 'No, I run an engineering firm with my partner,' I stuttered. And I act a bit, comedy mostly. Do a bit of writing here and there. Oh, and I've just started this website thing on parenting - you should check it out - it's great craic.'

And I...well my kid is in the same crèche as your daughter so obviously that means something, doesn't it? Like, that Jacob is in the crèche too because I need him to be because I'm really fucking busy on those days doing other things...ya know?

Ok, I didn't say that last bit out loud, to his face, because the tampon aisle is clearly no place for handbags at dawn. I sort of didn't know what to say to him at all, other than to list all the 'career' stuff I had going on. But besides 'work-work', I couldn't think of a single mam or dad I know who are 'People Of Leisure' since their kids came along. Do you?

As a quick example, here's a little diary I kept of a particularly balmy day around that September when I met the Dad, chronicling my 'leisurely' ladylike activities:

1.   I woke up at 3.30 a.m. to Jacob's screams and Ass Monkey's despair, 'I don't know what's wrong with him, he's been like this for an hour and a half! Please take over, for the love of God, please – I can't take it anymore!'. I did take over and finally got Jacob to lie down beside me in his bed and get over his tiny self at about 4.30 a.m.

2.   I woke up to a punch in the face from a tiny fist at 7.30 a.m. and then we were up. Jacob had pissed through his nappy and all his clothes, so after pulling all the sheets off his bed (more laundry for Mammy), he and I got into the shower together. I was ordered to count all of his rubber ducks and list them by colour, and then I spent ten minutes trying to stop him from throwing his toothbrush down the toilet.

3.   I checked on Pearl who had been at the vets the night before getting injections – still breathing. Phew. We all had a quick breakfast, Ass Monkey left for work, and I dropped Jacob to crèche.

4.   I nipped into the nearby beauty salon for a quick spray tan and nail paint for Ass Monkey's upcoming 40th birthday party. I had to suffer my big orange head getting stared at all day long, because the morning was the only time I could squeeze it in.

(FYI, normal ladies of leisure get that kind of thing done at nighttime under cloak of darkness and slip into bed unnoticed until they can wash off the excess in the morning, without anyone accusing them of blackface racism).

5.   I raced into town to get the last few items for said 40th party – managed to find everything I needed for everyone else, but failed to get myself even one thing on my own list because I ran out of time. Typical.

6.   Then it was over to the office to train our intern on our accounts programme for a few hours. Snooze fest for all parties concerned.

7.   I raced back to the house in a panic to make sure Pearl was still doing ok. I had been gone a little longer than I'd hoped for her. She greeted me at the top of the stairs (thank God), but she still wasn't 100% well. I spent two hours finalising decorations for the party, rang the vet and booked Pearl in to be seen again.

8.   She and I zoomed over to the vet where my lovely doggy proceeded to empty her arse of diarrhoea all over the vet table and then piss all over the floor. In front of a not unattractive veterinarian, may I add. Vetty Mc Dreamy, if you will. Pearl had to get two more injections so both she and I were obviously devastated when leaving.

9.   We sped back over to the crèche to pick Jacob up, where he was so excited to see me that he ran for me, instantaneously creaming himself against the corner of a shelf, and the girls and I spent fifteen minutes icing his bruised nose.

10.   The three of us eventually got home and it was straight up to the bath with Pearl first to de-shit her,

and then give Jacob his bath as normal (don't worry, he got fresh bathwater – we're not that kind of family). I dressed the beds with piss-free sheets and put all the laundry away. We nipped downstairs for dinner and cleaned the kitchen. Ass Monkey got in, put Jacob to bed and went back out again for beers (well it was his birthday weekend, so he was granted leave).

11.   After he left, I grimly discovered more of Pearl's shit in her doggie bed downstairs. I fired her blankets into the washing machine and the bed itself into the bath with bleach. I ironed shitloads.

Finished off decorating the chocolate truffles for Ass Monkey's party (I would like to mention that this took about an hour and then I subsequently forgot the bleedin' things for the party in the end). I disinfected all the floors where Pearl had shit and puked - the areas we knew about and the potential ones. Essentially, I disinfected every inch of floor space we had, to be sure, to be sure.

12.   I tried on my outfit for the party (I probably haven't mentioned that it was a Rockabilly theme so there was no getting away with rolling out the reliable LBD. Nope, actual effort had to be put in for this one). I inspected myself in the mirror: filthy looking with the increasingly deepening fake tan and crazy, crazy hair from all the running around. I quietly concluded that it would be grand once I got some make-up on and that I certainly was not too old for a 'Sailor Girl' outfit.

13.   I made myself a hot whiskey and got into bed where I had the first few quiet moments to myself to update my website for a few days. We're talking 1 a.m.

14.   Thought I'd do a 'Little Ones' check before a deep sleep which I knew was coming and that I really needed. Finalising everything for the big party the next day was going to require every single bit of energy that I could muster, and I'd probably need any extras from reserves too. Pearl was snuggled up on the bed beside me, fast asleep, and seemed marginally better.

I put a toe on the floor beside the bed to go check on the sleeping Jacob when I froze with fear: I could hear him stirring in the next room. He was awake…*Fuuuucccckkkk*….

So, to you, One Of The Dads From The Crèche Jacob Attended: what to say…what to say…

I'm a MOTHER. A lady of leisure?! Sure from the second I close my eyes to the second I open them, I'm working every minute. I'm a PARENT. There won't ever be time off again.

And by the way, you owe me a box of tampons, to fit an average vagina please.

Chapter Eighteen
MIDNIGHT BABY DRUGS RUN

I got to have one of those rare midweek nights, where Ass Monkey got home from work early enough to mind Jacob so that I could go to a show with some friends. Ordinarily, I miss stuff like that because of his working hours, unless we fork out for a babysitter, which doesn't always seem worth it.

Then there are the 'Sure We'll Wing It!' nights, the ones where you make vague plans to attend the event that all your mates are going to. On those occasions, the entire day goes swimmingly right up until the point that you are trying to leave the house and either end up dealing with a kid who is having a major shit fit for no reason, or a bloody something due to falling over when you were putting mascara on and were unable to stare at him expressly for those five seconds. Or your partner rushes in apologetically twenty minutes after you were due to leave and then it's too late to make it on time.

Any of the above generally results in my wanting to go to lie down in bed exhausted and not leave the house to attend the aforementioned event, which is undoubtedly nearly over anyway.

But on this night in particular, it all went to plan. Ass Monkey got in at a reasonable hour, Jacob was on his best behaviour, Pearl even offered to paint my toenails for the occasion. (Ok, obviously that's a lie, but could you imagine the hits on the YouTube clip?!)

I love going to shows, all sorts of them. I love theatre, music gigs, comedy, cabaret, performance art, poetry readings; you name it. If it's live, and it's arty, and especially if it involves nudity on any level, I am beyond thrilled (Side note: because I hosted a lot of burlesque and cabaret events over the last ten years, I have pretty much seen all my performer friends in the buff. As has Ass Monkey. At least, he's seen a lot of their boobies on stage at burlesque shows. Eventually, a boob is just a boob. Unless they are Sofia Vergara's in Modern Family. Even I can't keep my eyes off them. They are AMAZING).

The gig on this magical midweek night was a burlesque and vaudeville show from the States, and lots of the gang from the Irish burlesque scene were attending. We were all essentially craving fresh boobies. It was a blast – really old school, carney, beautiful costumes and a very funny host. We all had a great time.

At least I had a great time until afterwards, when I got outside and turned my phone on.

'S.O.S. BRING HOME BABY NUROFEN!' flashed up on my phone.

I checked the time – it was just after eleven. I was pretty sure that the chemist on Dame Street in the city was open until midnight so I shot over in the car.

Doors closed. *Shiiit*. Phone calls to and from home were getting a little more upsetting, as I could hear Jacob crying away in the background, who had a really high temperature and a sore throat.

'Have we seriously got no drugs in the house?!' I asked Ass Monkey.

'None. Not a Calpol, not a Nurofen, not even any of those suppositories that I still can't bring myself to administer' he replied.

Silence descended on our phone call, aside from, of course, poor little Jacob's constant wails in the background. He had been sick for three days and we hadn't topped up the baby drugs supplies. We were shit parents.

I got out of the car and went searching, keeping Ass Monkey on the line for updates and for the Anneka Rice-like dramatic effect of talking breathily whilst running, so my boys would know how serious I was about my mission.

'Jacob!' I yelled down the phone, running towards George's Street. 'Don't worry – I promise Mammy is going to get some drugs for you!'

I'm pretty sure two junkies, one prostitute and one lesbian headed for the nearby gay bar started following me at that point.

I burst into the Centra convenience store on the corner of Dame and George's Street, frantically searching all the shelves behind the counter.

'Seriously – they sell condoms here, whiskey, Gaviscon, paracetamol and any aerosol can you can think of – but no fucking baby Nurofen. What is wrong with this picture?' I shouted to Ass Monkey down the phone, trying to rack my brains for the next best plan.

'Ok, who do we know who has a baby who lives nearby? We need somebody who has a baby and some fucking drugs now!'

(Again, perhaps not the greatest of all things to be shouting about in public.)

However, as fate would have it, at that precise moment, I heard my name being called. I turned, and who did I see but my good pal Sorcha, who had just been on a night out with the girls and who recently had babba number two.

'Great to see you, you look amazing (she did), hope the babies are great....Em, any chance I can score some baby drugs off you?'

Cut to twenty minutes later and I was driving around the dark streets of Dublin City's Rialto area, trying to find Sorcha's house. She'd given her hubby the heads up that I was on the way, and I let Ass Monkey know that Super Mammy had it sorted.

As I pulled away from Sorcha and Kieron's house, with my half bottle of Baby Nurofen, a couple of suppositories and a handful of chamomile tabs, I thought about how lucky we are to know such great, generous people and how serendipitous it can be to live in Dublin sometimes. How lucky was it that I would have actually met the one person that I needed that night to help get Jacob back on track, temperature down and feeling well again? And who happened to live right on my way home?!

Chugging the car quietly down the dark city streets, post midnight, back to our house with my stash, I had to think that it was a scene that might give *Love/Hate* a run for its money.
Let's call it 'Stair/Gate'.

**PS I'm told that Boots in Blanchardstown Village Old Shopping Centre opens until midnight.
**PPS I'm also told that Tesco in Dundrum is 24 hours and sells Calpol.
**PPPS We currently have three bottles of Calpol, four bottles of Baby Nurofen and a box of those suppositories we're afraid of in our kitchen cupboard at all times.

Chapter Nineteen
INFANT-INDUCED ALCOHOLISM

My name is Sharyn Hayden and my baby makes me drink.

You know, before I had Jacob and became a mammy, I used to like to party. Oh, and dance. I used to love to dance. I'd be that girl, who was still up at 7 a.m. at some party or other in Ibiza, dancing my ass off, while all the others who had gone to the trouble of taking energy-promising drugs were fading in crumpled heaps on balconies, clutching on to the crotch of their PVC hot-pants for dear life (I witnessed a lot of people pissing themselves in those days. PVC is notoriously non-absorbent).

Eventually, lonely and exhausted in my quest for dance floor companions, I would head for bed, somewhere around the same time that the respectable residents of Ibiza were bringing their children to school. With smudged make-up, a see-through neon yellow bikini and scuffed silver-sprayed wedge runner boots, walking the streets back to one's own package-holiday apartment wasn't ever really an option at that point. And even without having children of my own to worry about, I was still normal enough in my twenties to not want to frighten the life out of the poor things.

I had long discovered at this juncture in my life, that a gay man who has taken three pills and smoked several million joints during the early hours of the dawn, is the perfect bedfellow in this type of situation and I would duly locate one to crash beside. It follows simple logic really:

1. There was no fear of said gay man waking up for at least ten hours so a full, uninterrupted sleep was guaranteed.
2. There was also no fear of them risking a sneaky hand-down-the-pants at any point so a full, uninterrupted sleep was guaranteed.

Although I never took drugs (and believe me, it was really hard not to when on holiday in Ibiza), drinking was my thing!

I loved booze – pints of Guinness, rum and Cokes, cocktails, wine, whatever I could get my hands on. Booze has contributed to countless great conversations that I may or may not ever remember, much dance floor madness and accidents (I once suffered a sprained ankle as a result of a very serious dance-off), outrageous sexual encounters with ridiculous people, sing-songs, rows, make ups, meeting new friends, and on one occasion, a public weeing of oneself.

Oh, and there was that time I got tequila poisoning…that was an extremely difficult Day After, let me tell you.

But now that I've had Jacob, my previously happy relationship with booze has gone a bit awry, and there are two major areas of concern to consider.

The first is that I've simply lost the knack: if I sit down to watch a movie with Ass Monkey after say, 9 p.m. when Jacob has gone to bed and get a glass of wine into me, I can guarantee you that I will be asleep by 9.45. Guaranteed. It would seem that the energy of yesteryears' Ibiza days are long gone.

The second area is slightly more disturbing. I've given this a lot of thought and have concluded that the idea of dealing with a frightened, distressed or suddenly sick child during the night with the 'Mammy's Had A Few' head, doesn't quite sit well with my moral conscience.

It's a sad and sorry day that I have to admit this but...

...it would appear that I've grown up.

Unless...unless my mother takes the baby overnight and promises to drive him back to our home herself, but not until lunchtime the next day. As in, I am gifted the opportunity to not only get as drunk as I please, but I also don't have to drive anywhere the next day. That is a very unusual occurrence and one that I totally and utterly would make the most of.

This 'gift' has to date been received one time since Jacob was born and I can report back that my mental state deteriorates from responsible-ladylike person to full-on teenage regression in a matter of seconds upon transfer of said baby.

My brain essentially tricks itself into believing that it and I am a willy-nilly single lady, free as a bird, and any recollection of being a parent goes out the window. The addition of unprecedented levels of booze, shoved down one's gullet, 100% contributes to this metamorphosis.

If you will, I shall now paint you a picture of the flashbacks I had in the weeks that followed that one night out, which was simply to attend a friend's music gig in the city. They are thus:

I fondled young boys' bums; young women's boobies; I ate ridiculous amounts of sour jellies which must have contributed to the alcohol-related sugar in my bloodstream tenfold; I met my friend's brother-in-law and couldn't remember his name; I confused another friend's baby daddy with someone else entirely; I offered to officiate at a lesbian's wedding with my online certification and worst of all – I flashed my arse to everyone at the venue.

By 4 a.m. that night/following morning, Ass Monkey and I were in a pizzeria in town where they were having what can only be described as the coolest disco where pizza is served, ever.
People were shoving slices of pepperoni and cheese into their faces and bouncing around to the latest Rihanna.
'It's like being in Ibiza, baby! Wooo!' I screamed as I ordered my slice and joined the party.

There is a very good chance that if the pizzeria had stayed open until 7 a.m., kept serving pizza and maybe just one or two delicious cocktails, that I would have stayed and replicated my Ibiza heydays.

I was ill for two full weeks afterwards. For the first seven days, I couldn't drink a hot drink of any kind because it felt like my throat was on fire.

Somewhere around Day Three, I remembered the Jägerbombs that we had necked – lots of them. Some time in the second week, photos of my stripper ass started circulating around the Internet. If I was still twenty-three and working in Planet Hollywood, this wouldn't have been so bad, but now on top of The Fear, I had the Mammy Guilts too.

Surely, a respectable mother shouldn't have been carrying on in such a manner, having so much fun and acting like such a...such a... well, such a Kerry Katona. Right?

(PS: it was a fucking great night).

Chapter Twenty
LICKING TIM MINCHIN

There are times when your kids let you down. I'm only 42% sure they're unaware of what they are doing while they're wrecking your plans/day/dinner/opaque tights with their Velcro shoes, so let's attempt to be the grown-ups here and assume that they're not doing it on purpose, shall we?

It is becoming more and more apparent, as Jacob nears the age of two and beyond that my life is definitely no longer the same.

For a good year and a half after he was born, I fought the invisible 'independent mother' battle with myself and Ass Monkey, and anyone else who would listen: fighting for my right to have my own life outside of my new 'job' as mother, fighting to keep working ridiculous hours, fighting to see my friends if and when I so chose to do so, fighting to get back to normal.

But I'm really not independent any more. I no longer have the freedom to skip out of bed when my body decides to wake itself, hop into the shower, nip down to the kitchen for a quiet cup of coffee and a read of the papers, stroll casually into town to meet a friend for a boozy lunch. In fact, as I write this, I realise I haven't read a paper cover to cover or had anything resembling a boozy lunch since Jacob was born.

Believe me, I've tried. I've gone through the motions of buying the Sunday papers, hoping against hope that some miracle might ensue that involves a team of house cleaners, ironers, make-up artists and hairdressers, and an energetic matronly-type lady (I picture Brenda Fricker – ample bosom, respectable in a floor-length dress, dependable and unlikely to run off with anyone that you thought YOU were shagging) - who will do all the housework (silently, invisibly and with a bra on, of course), as the nanny takes Jacob away to learn how to speak Chinese for two hours, and I salivate over the style section of The Sunday Times.

But alas, that has yet to happen. Normally, I can get through the first few pages 'unsupervised' and am just getting my teeth into the 'What's Hot and What's Not' section (approximately two-and-a-half pages), when I am dragged away to a 'crisis' that can vary in perceived levels of importance from 'Look! Daddy Pig fell in the water!' to 'I have poo in my eye.'

All of which, as any two-year-old will tell you, needs Mammy's attention STAT (They do need Daddy's attention too, of course, but for some reason, the Little One has chosen me as his very first point of complaint).

There are other times when my efforts to control schedules and routines, in an attempt to reduce the possibility of said child interfering with my life, are met with that child ultimately interfering with my life in much more spectacular fashion. There's no getting away with it.

Say, for example, you'd like to leave the house at 1.15 for a lunch date and so you plan your kid's nap at 12 for an hour. That means that said kid will either,

A) Refuse to go to sleep at the planned time (because they know you really, REALLY want them to), instead falling asleep at the ridiculously late hour of 12.45 and having to be dragged back up at 1 p.m., dressed while they're still half asleep - which takes an infinitely longer amount of time because of a lack of any sort of cooperation – and thus ensuring that you do not get on the road until at least 1.40 p.m.

Your kid will also almost certainly do a poo while you're en route, which is when you'll realise that you forgot the nappies and have to either turn back for home or stop at a shop along the way.

Whatever you choose, the lunch date will now have moved from 1.30 to 2.15 p.m., and the friend you are meeting will have to be back at their job (that you are so jealous of right now) by 2.30 p.m. and so the entire escapade is both embarrassing and pointless. You basically just end up having lunch with your kid. Just the two of you. Again.

OR,

B) Refuse to go to sleep altogether, resulting in the shittest tired-induced mood of all time. He will throw forks of bright orange food at your friend's beautiful cashmere jumper, shout things like 'I want my froggy' in an exorcist-esque voice (where did that come from?!), tell the entire café that their beans and chips are 'Esssgusting' and almost certainly do a poo while you're there.

Your friend, in this instance, will go back to the office early and vow never, ever, ever to have children and feel really sorry for you, but not sorry enough to invite you and your kid to lunch again.

When Jacob was really small, around six months, I attended a funeral for a good friend's brother who had suddenly passed away. The man was very young; it was an extremely sad situation, and the church was absolutely packed.

Rather than bring a buggy, I carried Jacob and a changing bag with a few essentials to keep him occupied and hopefully, quiet, during the mass. I made sure that he had a good nap and was well fed before we left, but he still had his own plans, even then. When the church music played, he was absolutely fine and quiet and very interested in listening to the sounds, but when it was quiet, i.e. when the priest or a family member was speaking, he kicked off. Yes, yes, precisely during the very sad moments when you're hoping that he'd be the most quiet.

So...I gave him another bottle. It kept him going for the five or so minutes it took him to drink it (he was a guzzler), and we got through to the end of the mass, just about. There were a few pleading

'Shushes' from our pew neighbours, but nothing major.

Afterwards, I approached my friends' parents to offer my condolences and give them a hug – there were many people who were doing the same thing so we lined up and waited our turn until we could eventually get to them. And right there, in the middle of the church and a gigantic throng of mourners – Jacob puked.

It wasn't just any old puke – but one of those unbelievable entire-contents-of-the-bottle-back-up-in-projectile-vomit-style pukes. One little burp emanated from his tiny body and every last drop of those five ounces or so was all back out again.

To add insult to injury, babies never, ever puke politely into their nappy bag or discreetly behind a mass booklet like you might hope – they like to puke RIGHT ON YOU. And as we were at a funeral, I was naturally wearing a long black coat, which was now completely drenched in regurgitated white baby formula down one side.

I just stood there, stunned into frozen position, not knowing what to do. Feeling a hand on my arm, I turned to see an elderly lady smiling at me. She gently led me out of the crowd and down to a small room at the back of the church, where some other ladies who helped with the mass were congregated. One took Jacob off my hands and cooed at him as two others led me to the bathroom.

Each of those ladies took a damp towel to my coat and rubbed as I stood there in between them with my arms outstretched, until it was clean again. I was so minded by them, it was like standing in your granny's kitchen having your face wiped with a mixture of smelly tea-towel and old lady spit. It was glorious and one of a very few times I regretted not being a Catholic.

And there are more stories just like that one. Loads more.

Of course, the mere fact that you have a child and are exhausted most of the time as well as on duty very early every day, means that they can be a buzz kill even when they're not around.

Nights out are limited because the entire time, you think to yourself *This is SO not going to be worth it tomorrow. I have to go home to sleep. I have to go home to sleep. I have to go home to sleep.*

In this instance, the mates that you are socialising with will fall into one of two categories:

1. The Sympathetic 'No-Worries-Sure-I-Could-Do-With-An-Early-Night-Myself' type.

And,

2. The 'I-Don't-Give-A-Fuck-Get-This-Shot-Down-Your-Neck' type.

I've been out with both. I once went on an accidental all-day bender with an old friend who didn't have kids. She was totally outraged that I absolutely had to call it a day at 1 a.m., insisting 'one for the ditch', 'another for the ditch', 'I promise, this last one for the ditch.' We'd been out since about half four that afternoon (a total rarity, I swear!)

She had been complaining about her other friends who had allowed their lives to be curbed by becoming new parents, that she couldn't get them out any more and wasn't I great that I was 'different.' The fact that this was our first time out together in about a year was clearly lost on her.

Anyway, I texted her the next day, when I was absolutely fucking dying, to say that if she loved me, she would come and help me mind Jacob for a couple of hours. Her response was, 'Ha Ha you're so funny! No thanks! That's your problem!'

I guess my pal was too busy lying in bed, PJs still on inside out from the night before, smoking her head off, drinking cure after whiskey cure, watching all her favourite shows on TV and possibly texting one of 'those' buddies to come and ride the hangover off her.

That was the kind of Day After that I too was in need of. Instead, I tried not to let the Peppa Pig theme music infiltrate my pounding brain and felt guilty all day for being a shit mother who had no energy to properly engage with Jacob. I couldn't even take him outdoors. Because the outdoors was too bright and too loud and too *outsidey*.

But therein, I think, lies the answer to the differences that occur in friendships when one has kids and the other doesn't. It isn't just one side of the friendship that changes – everybody changes.

Those who have kids should stay in touch with the friends who don't as much as possible and those who don't have kids should try to pretend as though they still like their friends as much as they did before they had kids, when they were still able to snog inappropriate ginger men for cocaine at Electric Picnic. Err, for example...

We should all at least try to tolerate each other's lifestyles and meet somewhere in the middle, shouldn't we? No one went off and had kids 'and ended the friendship' on purpose. Sometimes new parents think that their mates are having all the fun without them, posting Facebook photos of themselves straddling cowboys at a Texas rodeo, while their own photos are of baby cardigans with one arm longer than the other and a caption that reads: 'Did anyone else try this pattern and come up with the same results? I don't know what I've done wrong. PMSL!'

And equally, I have to concede that mates who don't have kids don't have to relate to the little persons who are now invading their once unattached friends' houses. They just have to randomly ask after their welfare – if that has to be accompanied by a faraway, slightly insincere look, then that's fine.

The parentals will have precisely the same look when they try to recall the Texan cowboy's name as you recall all seventeen sex positions that you experienced with him. You BITCH.

When I think about it, I have some old friends who don't know Jacob at all, some who see him weekly, some whose kids I never spent any time with when I was busy living my single life; some friendships are stronger than ever and some are lost forever. That's just life.

Not long after Jacob was born, shell-shocked, tired, elated, deflated – I had a night out planned with Ass Monkey. Wildly excited, he had bought us tickets to see Australian musical comedian Tim Minchin live at Vicar Street in Dublin. Having been a fan since my brother introduced me to Tim's hilarious song 'Inflatable You', I couldn't believe my luck and was more than a little giddy at the prospects of seeing him in the flesh.

You see, not only am I a fan of his musical and comedic talents, but there is also something verrrry attractive about him, with his little bare feet, painted fingernails, black eyeliner-painted eyes and his ginger dreadlocks...oh wait, that's it. I love him because he's a fellow ginger! (And he has an Aussie accent, AND he's a musician – swoon, double-fucking-swoon!)

I had it on good advice from someone I knew working at the venue (again, not the owner, more like the jacks cleaner. They know everything), that Tim would be signing some merchandise after the show for a select few people who got in line to wait for him.

As we drove to the show that evening, I planned every moment of our Big Meeting: what I was going to say to him and how we were going to be instant best friends upon clasping eyes on each other, and how Tim would of course agree to any private performances that I might request over the next decade or so. EASY.

Because I hadn't drank for the duration of the pregnancy and a little bit afterwards, the couple of glasses of vino that I had during the gig went to my head fairly quickly. I didn't drink much, but on reflection, I didn't need to, to get piddled. I was completely out of practice and my body wasn't quite yet ready or able for it.

I have some super-cringy memories of screaming like a wild woman at the end of each of Tim's songs, on my wobbly feet and waving my whole post-baby body at the direction of the stage, wolf whistling and generally ogling the poor man (Oh and yes, right next to Ass Monkey. He is very understanding, I agree).

However, none of the memories are more cringe-inducing than when I actually met the man. As I neared the top of the queue for the meet and greet and could see Tim in all his Technicolor glory, the excitement and nerves became all too much for me.

I was breaking out in a bit of a giddy sweat, and I couldn't tell if I needed to pee or was just horny.

(I was able to see his actual black eyeliner at this point, you understand. There is something about it on a man, on a ginger man... *shivers*...)

The lady in front of me had hogged him for long enough. Be gone with you! I thought to myself. It's time for a little Shaz-On-Tim action.

She slivered off eventually and there he was, glorious, standing in front of me with a halo of ginger all around him, bright as the daytime set of *Neighbours.*

I scrambled around my brain for the funniest thing I had planned, my one-line opener that would ensure our best-friendship/unconsummated romance for the rest of our lives. And drew a total blank. I couldn't think of a single decent thing to say to him.

Like a four-year-old showing her teacher the picture that she had just finger-painted, I thrust Tim's own programme and album that I had purchased at the merchandise stand for him to see, as if to say 'Look at me, I support the arts! I bought some stuff off you!'

Then I opened my mouth. Terrible, terrible mistake.

'I carried a watermelon!' I screeched at him.

La Minchin naturally looked very confused.

'Pardon?' he asked.
'Oh, em, you know, I thought it would just have been so funny to say that, you know, because I was excited to see you, and that's what you say when…you know *Dirty Dancing?*'
'Oh riiiiighhhtttt.'

Tim had no fucking idea what I was talking about, and why would he? He rightly ignored my weirdo fan self and got busy not making direct eye contact with me while he signed the programme and CD cover. I can only assume on reflection that he hoped I'd shut the fuck up and disappear as quickly as possible. Poor Tim.

'Can I lick your face?' I blurted out.

Again, he looked borderline terrified.

'Em, sure,' he managed. 'I mean, I wouldn't recommend it but okaaay.'

I didn't take note of the terror in his eyes, I didn't check myself and think that maybe I should remember any ladylike qualities that I still possessed and tell him I was just kidding – and that of course I didn't want to lick his face.

No, no. I grabbed his chin and slowly, deliciously, licked Tim Minchin's face.

Yep. If you don't believe me, my trusted sidekick Ass Monkey was kind enough to record my moment of mortification for me. And uploaded it to YouTube. The dote.

Chapter Twenty-One
SNATCH TO THE WIND

I would like to introduce the *'Snatch To The Wind Awards'*. It will be a really plush affair, in some swanky hotel where our kids/bosses/nosy neighbours and non-stop-knocking-on-the-door charity workers can't reach us, and our mobile devices are forbidden (lest anyone should try and reach us in search of the remote control or baby wipes, you understand. 'Erm, LOOK HARDER FFS!!').

We will drink champagne from pint glasses and wear ballgowns with no knickers on underneath. Some sexy bitch or other, such as the actress who plays Shane in The L Word, Lena Dunham or, oh fuck it, MERYL STREEP will be the main host for the evening. Meryl will, of course, be paid vast sums of money for doing the hosting in character as Anna Wintour from The Devil Wears Prada.

She will also be required to deliver killer one-liners from the script, such as 'By all means, move at a glacial pace. You know how that thrills me' every time that someone has to get up on stage to accept an award. Oh how we will drunkenly laugh.

The sole purpose of this evening, ladies and gentlemen, will be to celebrate and reward, Amazing Vaginas.

(Side-note: I don't think my vagina has ever received an award in its own right before. I mean sure, it's been popular in several categories, for example:

- **The Late Teens Experimental Years**
- **The New York I Think I'm Madonna And So Therefore Should Express Myself Through My Sex Era**
 - **The Mid 20s I'm Working And Have Money To Be Drunk A Lot So Will Shag Lots Of Idiots Years,**
and of course, not to forget my *absolute* favourite, the
- **I've Just Turned 30 And Am Freaking Out So Must Shag All The 21-Year-Olds Stage**.

I still think though, God love her, that even during all of that, my vagina was really and truly only being given a 'Supporting Vagina' role – no lead parts, and certainly fuck all control over the script or direction her career was going in.

Sure, the rider was basic enough, covering official health checks, smear tests, nice lingerie and de-fuzzing treatments at the salon, but really, the overall management was way off.

And as for respect and equality in the workplace? I can tell you that my vagina was several times in a position whereby she should have taken a case at the labour courts.

At the Snatch To The Wind Awards, there will be no 'Supporting Vagina' awards on offer, only main prizes - big prizes - for each of the categories, which will include:

1.   Outstanding   Vagina   in   The Arts/Medicine/Science Award (all careers will of course be included. I am still undecided on the 'Outstanding Vagina In The Porn Industry' category, because I think the judges' work would be pretty much cut out for them. From what I've seen, those girls have some of the most robust vaginas on the planet. How could they possibly choose the best one?).

2.   The **Holy Vaginal Matrimony** Award – for the best speech from a woman at a wedding, straight or gay. I don't know how many weddings I've attended now where the bride doesn't say a word – not a word – WTF?!

3.   The **I Can't Believe It's Not Vagina** Award – for a fabulous new sister from the transgender community.

4.   The **I'm A Vagina, Get Me Out Of Here!** Award – dedicated to someone who got the fuck out of that shit job/nasty relationship/the queue at Ikea on a Sunday afternoon in search of a better life.

5.   The **Look Up, It's Vagina** Award – for outstanding work in ignoring the 'men can do it just as well as you but will be paid infinitely more cash for their troubles' and kicking ass in their chosen business.

Mmmm, I think that could be it for now. Sure I could go on, but we'd be there all night, the champagne might run out, and if left at home to one's own devices for long enough, 'someone' is likely to have used the fur on the family dog's back to wipe one of our children's arses in lieu of being able to locate the frickin' baby wipes.

In my modest personal opinion, this would be a far more sophisticated and vaginal-driven way to celebrate our vaginas for all the great work they do, than this latest weird trend of soliciting 'Push Presents' from our guilt-ridden and put-upon partners. Why the actual fuck should we demand an over-priced, often pointless, item for the notion of 'going to the trouble' of giving birth?

It just seems so ludicrous not to consider that we elected to do this together, this baby-making thing. Yes, one of us knew we would be the 'Luggage Holdall' part of the deal, but presumably had a fair notion of what all that entailed when we signed up?

Even the phrase 'Push Presents' sounds wrong. It conjures up less images in my mind of women giving birth to another human being, but more imagery of Rihanna dry-humping the floor in a dollar sign-decorated bikini, if I'm honest.

And what about those who don't 'push' a baby out – what about all those amazing women who endure C-sections? What about our friends and family who foster/adopt/choose surrogacy – are they forbidden from this elite notion?

Even though Jacob technically came out of my own vagina, I can't truly say that I did much 'pushing'. First of all, I was drugged up to the eyeballs with the epidural – TO THE EYEBALLS (ok, well technically, up to somewhere around the waist)

– but the point is, I didn't even feel like I was pushing, or doing much of anything when Jacob was being delivered.

I had one sneaky eye open on Ass Monkey who I was laughing at because his 'jobs' were to press one of my legs somewhere up around my earlobe and make sure that I didn't push with my eyes (my mother reported to have burst a few blood vessels in her eyelids giving birth to one or other of us from pushing too hard, so I was determined not to let that happen to me).

Ass Monkey was taking his role so seriously that his hands had actually gone a bit purple from holding on to my leg so tight (whereas meanwhile I couldn't feel a thing), and his tired eyes were like saucers staring at my eyeballs to make sure they didn't pop out of my head. And next thing we knew, Jacob was arriving into the room and the world, and I couldn't tell you that I had anything to do with helping that. When your bits are numb, your bits are numb. Did I push, really? Who knows.

Furthermore, when I went for a check-up with my doctor a couple of months later, she informed me that 'no one would ever know you had a baby'. My episiotomy scar was healed, my Kegel exercises had strengthened everything back up - I could essentially, if I so desired (?!), deny any knowledge of having given birth to the little man. So why all the fuss over my 'poor vagina' who had to do all this pushing? She wasn't complaining.

I had a very educational conversation on the matter with some friends I went to school with – all hard-working women, mind – who described the 'Push Presents' they received as ranging from

Manolo Blahniks that they were unlikely to ever wear, to Prada handbags, iPads and diamond bracelets!

A quick search on any internet search engine of the term will throw up articles on the gross excesses that the likes of Kim Kardashian received for giving birth to her long awaited child (a $500,000 ring by the fucking way), to websites completely dedicated to selling a full range of push presents.

Jewellery, designer items, spa breaks away – you name it, they have your partner's guilt in their hands and they will happily charge you big wads of cash to alleviate it somewhat.

In defiance of this madness, I have compiled a list of what I think would be some much more useful, touching, and overall 100% appreciated gifts from your loved one when you welcome a new baby into the house:

1.   A   voucher   for   a   daily   ten-minute shoulder/back/foot rub. This may or may not include a Happy Ending, that shall remain the ultimate   decision   of   the   bearer   of   the feet/back/shoulders.
2.   The employ of early-morning staff, akin to the ones 'downstairs' in Downton Abbey, who will quietly sort out the cooking and cleaning while you're asleep, lay out a puke-stain-free, matching outfit for you to wear at the end of your bed, and disappear as soon as you surface.
3.   Written documents outlaying the understanding that She Who Is Breast Feeding will not have any further demands put on her boobs by anyone other than the baby for a fixed period of time.

4.   A contract detailing the removal of unhelpful in-laws, outlaws, neighbours, friends etc., when the unease of either partner is expressed. There should be no boundaries to this gift, i.e. the removal can be enforced at any time or place, even at a baptism or birthday party, and can include the use of brute force if necessary.

5.   A voucher for a photo shoot that will feature all members of the family, not just one partner plus child plus the other partner's foot/half a hand/blurry side profile.

6.   A little holiday – it doesn't have to be expensive, it doesn't even have to be abroad. Just somewhere to go together for the weekend, or overnight, where you can bond with each other and talk to each other and make plans together about the type of parents you want to be. Preferably, this retreat will be somewhere that the internet doesn't work, so you can't check any work emails or social media pages. It should be pure, uninterrupted, dedicated family time.

7.   A 'Pretend Who Is Asleep The Longest' outright BAN. If the child or children are in need of their parents during the night, there will be a grown-up, mature discussion between both parents outlining their cases for and against being the one to get up out of bed. There will be no ridiculous attempts at pretending that their screams can't be heard and P.S. NOBODY can fake snore.

8.   A guarantee that everyone will be up to speed on the correct nappy sizes and type of formula/number of ounces required at all times. Phone calls from one parent to another enquiring as to the answer to this exact type of information will not be tolerated.

9.   Consent that the repeated loss of the kitchen sink plug is neither helpful nor believable.

10. Agreement that it would be better to put a puke-stained bed sheet straight into the washing machine rather than leaving it out on the line 'to dry first' and then forgetting about it for a week, while the neighbours wonder just what the fuck is wrong with you.

11.   The painting of The Bedtime Rules somewhere helpful in the house. This can be pasted in blood on the landing walls if necessary, so that no one parent or another can 'innocently forget' that a child does not need to watch seventeen episodes of Peppa Pig back-to-back during the hours of 6 p.m. and 9 p.m.

12.   A Box of Quiet Kindness and Helpfulness. This box should be opened every single day and let loose on the home, so that the primary caretaker of this newborn house-and-heart-wrecker can have a quiet environment to work in, can sleep if they need to sleep, can cry if they need to cry, can get out for a walk if they need a walk, can be reassured that they're doing a great job, can take ten minutes to get washed and dressed in the morning, can have an afternoon to themselves here and there to go to the salon or shops, can be promised the presence of a partner who thinks they're amazing and knows that they're still a human being with needs and wants outside of being a parent and….

…too much? Yeah I thought so.

Fuck it, just get me the Manolos.

Chapter Twenty-Two
TWO

As Jacob has now reached his second birthday, I have been reflecting on everything that has happened in our lives since his arrival. It's been BATSHIT CRAZY, that much I know. I thought my life was busy and a little left of centre before he burst onto the scene, but his resultant presence thereafter has been nothing short of a whirlwind.

Simultaneously setting up our own business while becoming parents for the first time could probably be described as a form of self-harm, but the stress and strain of it is now beginning to pay off. We have more than one van on the road now, and an official office and workshop so that our home no longer has to house bits of broken machinery and Revenue reminders and staplers and Tipp-Ex on the kitchen table.

We have help with great staff and I have to actually leave the house to go to work, which is far healthier than trying to cram everything in during the eight blissful minutes of peace I have when Jacob is watching *Bob The Builder*.

Now that business is all set up, I've finally conceded that I can't do it all. I can't leave the house at 6 p.m. for a comedy show that will have had me on edge with the planning of it for weeks, only to upset both Ass Monkey and Jacob by being unavailable for that most precious of things – bedtime – and then make minus €35 on the door because no one bloody well showed up anyway.

I've taken my creative outlets elsewhere – to writing during the day when I'm not at the office and online at the Raising Ireland website. I'm learning so much from all the parents out there who are raising kids and pets, and businesses, and building homes, and doing charity work, and partying when they can, and looking amazing while they do it and it is great to know that we're all in this rocky, leaking, slightly exhilarating paddle boat together…

…and I know how hard it all can be. I can freely admit that I have cried more in the last two years than I ever did my entire life.

Exhaustion, worry about keeping this little baby alive, disappointment in the cruelties of life, both personally and in business, stress from the glare of the work computer in the living room, guilt for running to work on something the second the baby closed his eyes, agitation at the sound of unannounced visitors knocking at the door because there was so, so much to be done when I should have been so, so glad of the company.

And I do regret it to a degree, to not have been more present and more relaxed when Jacob came along. That I didn't stay in my pajamas and tell the visitors to make their own f*cking coffees, or to leave when I was tired. That I didn't ask for, or accept more offers of help when I could have had it. That I gave so much of a shit what the stupid house(s) looked like.

I've learned a lot about myself in the last two years, and the biggest of all the lessons is this: I need to chill the fuck out.

The flip side of all this is guilt and hard feelings, that while I never cried so much, I have never laughed and smiled so much either. No matter how tired or cranky or stressed out I have been, Jacob can give me one of his 'I hope you know that I am taking the absolute piss out of you right now, Mammy' smirks, and I am on the floor laughing in seconds.

Things are much different now that we are somewhat 'out the other side'– there were times when Ass Monkey and I weren't sure we'd make it, on any level, but we've survived the baby years with Jacob (and let's not forget Pearl!), the first years of a new business, two house moves, family illnesses, bereavement, fights, sleeping in the back of a van at the Electric Picnic music festival, not to mention all of my shows and auditions and shoot days that I throw in for the FUN…

…so I'm pretty sure we can now survive anything.

I always loved the bones of Jacob, but these days, I am enjoying myself around him more. I put fewer demands on myself, other than to show him a good time in this world while he's in my company.

The last two years have been spectacular, in every way, and I am now looking forward to the next two minutes, two hours, two months, with a big smile on my face because he is with me. Everything else can – and should – stand still.

Photograph By Graciela Vilagudin

conclusion
ON THE WAY OUT

Oh life, you crazy bitch. You're a funny and wondrous thing aren't you? Sometimes we forget that you're constantly happening all around us and do silly things like spend hours wasting time watching Keeping Up With The Kardashians re-runs on the E! Network. (That is what's commonly known as Time You Will Never Get Back, by the way. Like, why do those grown women all speak in baby voices?!)

Other times, we check in and really enjoy you, catching ourselves singing along to the radio, or emitting a proper, genuine outward laugh when in the company of someone we love. Those are the times when you realise 'Oh fuck – I'm *happy*. When did that happen?!'

My favourite ever moment, and reminder about the beauty of life and people, came to us when Jacob was a tiny baby. We were in a packed local coffee shop as I was in search of a cuppa and a slice of cake getting handed to me by someone who would also wash up the dishes afterwards.

An elderly couple, easily in their late seventies or early eighties, arrived soon afterwards and couldn't find anywhere to sit. Not one able-bodied adult male or female paid them the slightest bit of notice as they stood awkwardly in the doorway so I beckoned them over and got them to squeeze in beside us.

'We've been coming here every Wednesday morning on the bus from town for two years,' the elderly lady told me. 'For tea and toast.'

We had great chats as they told me how they picked up their pensions from the post office each week and took the bus together for their little weekly date to this particular coffee shop by the seaside. Afterwards, they went for a walk along the promenade. The man was a bit stiff on his feet and the lady had a hearing aid but besides that, they seemed to be in fairly good health.

I thought they were adorable as they cooed over Jacob and asked me all about how he and I were getting on. When their tea and toast was consumed and they were leaving for their stroll, the elderly man did that lovely traditional thing of placing a fiver in the folds of Jacob's baby blankets, for luck.

Thinking of the pension they had just picked up, I protested,

'No, no, you don't have to do that, honestly!'

They wouldn't hear of my giving it back to them and as they departed, the elderly lady commented, 'He needs it more than we do. He's on his way in, and we're on our way out.'

And they smiled, waved and left for their walk. It was so beautiful. I still can't even type about it, never mind tell anyone the story in person, without welling up.

Although... that may be something to do with my current hormone levels.

See here's the thing – as of October 2013, it would appear that I forgot to take my pill at some point and....

HOLY SHIT WE'RE HAVING ANOTHER BABY!

ACKNOWLEDGMENTS

Ass Monkey – my Alan – puts up with a lot of shit from me. A LOT. Writers are probably the worst, moodiest fuckers in the world to live with. But he hasn't left me (yet) so for that, I am thankful. I love that ride of a man.

Love to my mum for teaching me how to parent with love, humour and a very clean toilet.

Love to my dad for feeding my creativity as a child with the best books and music, and for promising to never read this book (phew!).

To my three younger brothers - Shane, Eoghan and Noel – even though they think I'm a crazy feminist loudmouth, they'll buy this book anyway and use it to prop up a goal post somewhere.

I would never have written a single word of this book, or created RaisingIreland.com without the author, comedian and great friend, Carol Tobin. She is a total sexy bitch.

Every woman needs at least one good friend who is a little bit more pregnant than they are, so that they can report back from the front line. That friend for me is Nicola 'Simpsonite' Tarrant - I love her for never lying to me, for never letting me doubt myself and for never letting me quit drinking.

Thanks and love to the Fynes family for allowing me to steal Ass Monkey for myself!

To Sinead McCrone for proofreading this ranty manuscript while simultaneously pumping in a broom cupboard at work.

Huge thanks to Maeve Barry Communications for getting The Good Vagina Word out there, in beautiful style and humour as always - now go and organise your feckin' wedding, will ya?!

The wonderful Irish actress Clelia Murphy agreed to launch this book for me with this great response: 'I'm 97% sure it'll be fine. Like the pill…!' Legend.

Olive O'Brien at Creative Writing Ink edited this book and gave me invaluable advice and positive support along the way, so lots of love to her!

I am completely blessed to have an amazing and eclectic bunch of friends in my life; Rory Carrick, Eleanor Finn, Sue Bolger, Doireann Langford, Sophie McCrone, the Rush gang, The Pony Girls, Tracy Martin, Paddy Cullivan, The Maryfielders, Emma Howlin, The Planet Hollywooders and Luigi Maloners, Jennifer Stevens and Suzanne Rose, Marc Cleary, Amy Allen, Paul Ryder & Conor Behan, Paddy Shirley, Kieron and Sorcha Black, Cliona Dukes, Ciaran Bradley, Amanda Brunker, The DYTers, Siona Curtis, my sisters-in-law Nicola and Claire - I can't believe how lucky I am sometimes.

Vanessa O'Loughlin from Writing.ie has been fantastic in championing this book from its' humble beginnings, for no other reason than she loves what she does. How many people can say that?!

I want to say a huge thanks to all the parents, contributors and readers of RaisingIreland.com – your enthusiasm for my blog posts really inspires me to write with more and more gusto every day.

And finally – to my amazing Jacob. Thanks for your tantrums, for your kisses, for your wee through my sheets in the middle of the night. You're my favourite person in the entire world xxx

ABOUT THE AUTHOR

Aside from her work at RaisingIreland.com, Sharyn Hayden also contributes as a guest blogger at popular Irish parenting site HerFamily.ie. Her short story *The Boss* was published in 'The Little Book Of Christmas Memories' (Liberties Press).

When she isn't writing, Sharyn works as a jobbing actress and voiceover artist.

She lives in Dublin, Ireland, with her ever-expanding family and her collection of items that have not yet been ironed.

For more, visit **www.SharynHayden.com**

15316445R00113

Printed in Great Britain
by Amazon